Beyond the Tryline

Rugby and South African Society

Beyond the Tryline

Rugby and South African Society

Albert Grundlingh (signature)

**Albert Grundlingh,
André Odendaal
and Burridge Spies**

Ravan Press   Johannesburg

First published by Ravan Press
PO Box 145 Randburg 2125
South Africa

First published 1995

ISBN 0 86975 457 2

Cover design: Ingrid Obery, Ravan Press
Cover repro: Centre Court Studio
DTP: Luisa Potenza

Printed by Clyson Printers, Cape Town

*For our respective families, who have only a limited interest
in rugby, but allowed us the space
to complete this project.*

Above: Port Elizabeth, Thursday 30 July 1891. South African rugby players enter the international arena in the first test match against Britain.
*Photograph from **Toyota se Springbok Sage. Die Verhaal in Beeld van 1891 tot Vandag** by Chris Greyvenstein, Human and Rousseau, 1977.*

Below: South Africa's controversial re-entry, after years of isolation, into international rugby. On 15 August 1992 South Africa played New Zealand's All Blacks.
*Photograph courtesy **The Pretoria News**.*

Contents

List of acronyms

African National Congress (ANC)
African Political Organisation (APO)
Eastern Province Native Rugby Union (EPNRU)
Griqualand West Colonial Rugby Football Union (GWCRFU)
International Rugby Board (IRB)
Kwazekhele Rugby Union (KWARU)
National and Olympic Sports Congress (NOSC)
Pan-Africanist Congress (PAC)
South African African Rugby Board (SAARB)
South African Bantu Rugby Board (SABRB)
South African Council of Sport (SACOS)
South African Coloured Rugby Football Union (SACRFU)
South African Cricket Board of Control (SACBOC)
South African Native National Council
South African Non-racial Olympic Committee (SANROC)
South African Rugby Association (SARA)
South African Rugby Board (SARB)
South African Rugby Football Federation (SARFF)
South African Rugby Football Union (SARFU)
South African Rugby Union (SARU)
South African Soccer Federation (SASF)
South African Sports Association (SASA)
Western Province Coloured Rugby Football Union (WCRU)
Western Province Rugby Football Union (WPRFU)

Introduction

Rugby has gripped the imagination of a large section of South Africa's white males throughout the country's volatile 20th century political history. The game's pre-eminence is virtually unrivalled: 'Superlatives are usually reserved for rugby players, not actors or writers or even politicians'.[1] In their enduring fascination with the game, there has only been a difference in degree between white Afrikaans and English speakers; whereas English speakers are said to be fond of their rugby, Afrikaner nationalists are often thought to be passionate about it.[2]

This interest is reflected in many ways, one of them being the number of books which have chronicled the feats of the Springboks on the rugby fields of South Africa, New Zealand, Australia and the United Kingdom. But for all of that, we have only a limited under-standing of the deeper social significance of rugby for the different groups in South Africa and the historical process which account for the nature of the country's different rugby cultures.

Sport in society can be considered as a kind of 'deep play' in which the innermost and often hidden values of a culture can be detected. 'Sport is not only a physical activity; it has heroic and mythical dimensions and can be viewed as a story we tell ourselves about ourselves.'[3]

With this in mind, the chapters forming *Beyond the tryline* explore a range of questions. What are the connections between rugby, nationalism and class? What does rugby reveal about gender relations? What is the relationship between schooling and rugby? Did rugby ease race relations in South Africa, and can the game be regarded as a unifier? How important was rugby in the calculations of South African politicians? What has been the effect of greater commercialisation? There may not be definitive answers to all or any of these questions, but they have to be asked and answers attempted.

The book begins with an analysis of recent developments that led to South Africa's re-entry into international rugby, and debates the likely significance of the 1995 Rugby World Cup tournament for the country. It then moves, in contrast to the much-publicised World Cup, to the almost forgotten dimensions of black rugby and the range of influences that shaped the world in which black people played and organised rugby.

This is followed by a wide-ranging assessment of rugby as it evolved amongst white English speakers who had first brought the game to South Africa. A central feature of South African sport during the apartheid years was its gradual exclusion from international competition; responses from the state and the rugby fraternity to this development, and the enduring social and cultural significance of the game in a beleaguered white society, are therefore also analysed. Finally, in an attempt to understand Afrikanerdom's near obsession with the game, the interrelationship between rugby, nationalism and masculinity is probed.

These essays make no claim to present an exhaustive account of the sport in South Africa. But they do cast some light, in a way which has not been done before, on the contemporary and historical importance of rugby in South African society.

For some readers, references to groups like Afrikaners, English speakers, blacks or coloureds might have an 'old' South African ring. However, while these categories can be shown to be brittle, historically they had a certain cohesion which cannot be summarily wished away. Before the next World Cup tournament comes to South Africa, perhaps these terms will have lost much of their meaning and connotation.

Pretoria
April 1995

Notes

1 C. Laidlaw, *Mud in your eye: A worm's eye view of the changing world of rugby* (Cape Town, 1974), p. 188.

2. R. Archer and A. Bouillon, *The South African game: sport and racism* (London, 1982), p. 69.

3. R. Holt, *Sport and the British: A modern history* (Oxford, 1989), p. 3.

CHAPTER ONE

The new politics of rugby

Albert Grundlingh

On 2 February 1990 the incumbent state president, F.W. de Klerk, made what was probably the most important speech of any white South African leader in parliament: he formally unbanned the African National Congress (ANC) and other proscribed organisations. This effectively ended 30 years of exile for the country's major black political organisations.

A number of factors led to this landmark decision: international sanctions had debilitated the economy and restricted room for manoeuvring on the part of the state; internal insurrections placed further strain on the state as a recurring cycle of repression and resistance shaped the contours of South African society; armed attacks by the ANC, though never seriously extending the military, added to increased instability; and the international order had changed with the collapse of communism in Eastern Europe, leading the state to realise that it could no longer play the West off against the East.

The rocky road of rugby reconciliation

De Klerk's speech signalled the end of apartheid as official state policy. Although the negative social and economic effects of a discriminatory policy which had been entrenched for decades could not be erased by decree overnight, the fact that apartheid measures were to be scrapped from the statue books did open up the way for a fundamental restructuring of society. It also meant that the long-standing international sports boycott of South Africa could be re-assessed.

Rugby administrators welcomed De Klerk's announcement. Danie Craven, president of the South African Rugby Board (SARB), described it as a 'wonderfully encouraging move' which would facilitate South Africa's re-entry into international sport. Jan Pickard of the Western Province Rugby Board was even more optimistic and wasted no time in informing the public that 'they would be surprised to see which teams would come and tour without further ado in 1990.'[1] Other observers were more cautious and warned that the political influence of the National and Olympic Sports Congress (NOSC), affiliated to the ANC, should not be underestimated; until the various establishment and anti-apartheid sporting bodies were united under one banner and until it was clear that the dismantling of apartheid had become an irreversible process, the chances of foreign tours to South Africa were slim.[2]

This is not, however, the way Craven saw the situation in February 1990. He had an imperfect grasp of the magnitude of the change required in South Africa and this had a bearing on his failure to understand the precise linkages between rugby and politics. For Craven, the abolishment of apartheid primarily involved the scrapping of social and economic discriminatory practices. It did not entail a universal franchise, majority rule and a totally new political dispensation. Publicly, Craven made it clear that the 'government had to be very careful about the vote. There is one thing that the government must never do, and that is to give everybody an equal vote.'[3] He could see no reason why South Africa could not return to rugby as usual; apartheid, as far as he was concerned, was officially abolished and international tours could be resumed.[4] The fact that a new political order still had to be negotiated and that the transitional process was fraught with pitfalls and possible reversals was immaterial to him.

Sportspeople in anti-apartheid organisations had to take such political realities into account; sport has been an important weapon in their arsenal and to surrender it without being able to show tangible gains would have been politically unacceptable. The NOSC therefore resolved that establishment sporting bodies like the SARB should support the moratorium on sports tours and work together with anti-apartheid forces in eliminating all discrimination in sport before seeking fresh international ties. The SARB had to show its commitment to change. 'This is the time', it was argued, 'for the SARB to display its sincerity, to catch the moment'.[5]

The moment, however, meant different things for different people. Craven was in full agreement that one controlling body should be established – he had already had a discussion on this issue with the anti-apartheid South African Rugby Union (SARU) as early as 1977 and had also met the ANC in Harare in the late 1980s – but he baulked at the idea of a moratorium. Patel, of SARU, on the other hand, maintained that a condition for the unity talks between his organisation and the SARB was that the moratorium should be supported. SARU was deeply suspicious that the SARB was only interested in unity talks for the sake of expediency. The Rev. Arnold Stofile, junior vice-president of the SARU in 1990, warned that anti-apartheid sports people and administrators had to be 'vigilant not to be used as tools by the racists, as window dressing for international tours, or black-mailed into entrenching international tours.'[6] Stofile's call echoed a wider concern in the ANC during this period, namely, that in dealing and negotiating with the National Party government, the movement added greatly to the credibility of the government at home and abroad.[7] More than likely this stiffened SARU's resolve not to accede to international tours prematurely.

For the greater part of 1990 and well into 1991 a series of acrimonious exchanges between Craven and Patel followed. Exploratory talks between the two organisations ground to a halt amidst accusations and counter-accusations of intransigence, insensitivity and opportunism. Whilst other sporting codes managed to merge with relative ease, rugby remained the odd one out. 'Perhaps it is the aggressive nature of the game that causes rugby officials to fight', one journalist observed wryly.[8] But central to the *impasse* were two almost diametrically opposed perceptions of the role of sport in society. Craven tended to deny the social significance of rugby and consistently argued against what he considered to be outside interference in rugby matters. For the NOSC and SARU there was not such a stark dividing line between sport and society. Sport was seen as 'inter-linked with the total social formation' and had to 'reflect society'.[9]

It had now become clear that the 'warring bodies' were unable to establish common ground. In March 1991 Steve Tshwete, ANC sport spokesperson and current South African Minister of Sport, entered the fray. Tshwete was a keen rugby enthusiast and had played representative rugby in the Border area during the early 1960s. Apart from his sporting credentials, he had spent 15 years on Robben Island as a political prisoner and another 11 years in exile. While on Robben Island he had been involved in organising rugby competitions amongst his fellow prisoners.

Tshwete had gained a reputation as 'Mr Fix It' for his part in brokering talks between other sporting codes, most notably cricket. He regarded the establishment of one controlling body as being of paramount importance in countering sectionalism and of empowering previously disadvantaged sections of the population. It was therefore essential, he argued, for SARU and the SARB to 'get together so that they influence each other in a way that any hardened attitudes can be broken down'. Tshwete was also concerned about the perceived negative spin-offs which the rugby war had on wider South African politics. 'It is a delicate process', he said, 'where the rugby talks are bound to influence the political process in the country and *vice versa*, so that whatever is done, we should operate under this new body'. This was also the message he tried to convey to Craven, whom he found more 'attentive and not insensitive to the demands of the occasion'.[10]

There is also evidence that Craven had become increasingly aware that without the blessing of an organisation like the ANC as well as SARU, the SARB would find it difficult to organise an international tour without it being disrupted by demonstrations and violence. The 'rebel' English cricket tour of 1989-90, which had to be aborted mid-way because of mass demonstrations, was a stark reminder to Craven that the same could happen to rugby.[11] Craven was averse to being dictated to, but he was pragmatic enough to realise that, without some strategic re-positioning, South African rugby would not get back into the international fold.

Tshwete played a continuing part in steering the talks towards unity. Pressure was exerted on both Patel and Craven. A meeting was even arranged between Nelson Mandela, ANC president at the time, and Craven. This apparently further helped to smooth the way. In December 1991 it was announced that a new unified sporting body,

the South African Rugby Football Union (SARFU), would be launched early in 1992. The new body committed itself to the development
of rugby across the board and in particular in disadvantaged areas; at
the same time the go-ahead for international tours in 1992 was given.[12]
In the process SARU had to drop the moratorium on tours, but for the
first time in its history of more than a hundred years, the SARB had
to take the opinions and influence of people other than white seriously
and, moreover, act upon them.

While the SARB had coloured and black affiliates in the past, they
had never exerted the same pressure as Patel and SARU.[13] Now rugby
administrators faced up to each other as equals. An interim constitution, designed to underpin the unity process, ensured 50/50 representation for the SARB and SARU. Craven was to be joint president
with Ebrahim Patel, the latter to take over in 1993. Despite the
apparent equitable 50/50 agreement, it was an uneasy unity; both
parties were driven to it by circumstances rather than conviction.

Establishing a sense of unity in the boardroom, however shaky,
was one issue; ensuring that the policy was accepted and implemented
lower down the ranks, was another. In certain areas in the *platteland*
and in the Western Province pressure had to be applied to bring
recalcitrant white sub-unions into line. Incidents on the field underlined the difficulties of the merger. It was with considerable trepida-
tion that some clubs from predominantly white areas ventured into
often volatile African or coloured townships to fulfil their league
fixtures.

Although such fears were often without foundation, a few matches were indeed marred by unruly crowd behaviour and racial
animosity. In the Karoo town of Graaff Reinet, for instance, a game
between a white team from De Aar and the local coloured team had
to be abandoned before the end of the first half as 80 angry spectators
stormed onto the field, disagreeing with a decision from the referee
and threatening to attack the white team. 'Kill them, kill them', the
spectators were reported to have shouted. 'Today we will be looking
through the ribcages of the *boers*! We are going to necklace them.
Close the entrance gates so that we can show them who is the boss!'[14]
The referee sprinted to his car and the players rapidly retreated to the
change rooms. Similar incidents occurred in the Eastern Cape and on

5

occasion the police had to disperse the crowd with teargas.[15] In 'ordinary' rugby games players are often given to needling the opposition; it was too much to expect no flare-ups and racial baiting between players from communities which had long histories of antagonism.

An agreement that rugby would be promoted amongst the disadvantaged communities of South Africa was a key element in the process that led to unification. SARFU officially launched such a programme in March 1993. A sum of R13-million was spent in the first year and a great deal of activity marked the program: more than 116 000 young, predominantly African and coloured, rugby players attended clinics and coaching courses, and 6 000 coaches, 650 referees, and 1 772 administrators from all over the country were involved in arranging and supervising proceedings.[16]

With all the frenetic activity, the programme outwardly appeared to be off to a very satisfactory start. But appearances proved to be deceptive. Certain development efforts bordered on fiascos as a result of poor organisation. While some of this chaos can be put down to teething problems, internal bickering and jockeying for lucrative executive positions on the development committees were problems of a different order. 'Little men with nary a constructive thought, have to see to their livelihood – not latent talents', was one caustic verdict.[17]

The development programme faced enormous challenges. As a result of years of apartheid-induced neglect, rugby had to start from scratch in many townships. Extremely poor facilities were major obstacles. In certain areas people with as little conception of the game as the boys they were supposed to coach were appointed as coaches.[18] Moreover, there was some political undercurrent of resistance to rugby as a game associated with the police and apartheid.[19] The enormity of these problems raised the possibility that SARFU might lose heart and that the programme might backslide after the first flurry of activity.

Indeed, in 1993 some observers were of the opinion that with the World Cup in the offing, the development programme has lost much of its former urgency. Administrators, it was reported, viewed 'development as a necessary evil, and at best tolerated as with a naughty child. You know it's yours, but for heaven's sake, keep it at bay.'[20]

The programme did have some successes. The press was keen to give publicity to black youngsters who showed rugby promise, and it was almost as if the media was half-relieved at being able to report in a positive vein.[21] Perhaps more important than the number of black boys excelling at the game was the way in which the programme raised questions about the place of rugby in South African society as a whole. One journalist pointedly remarked:

> *It is hard to write about back row moves immediately after returning from a township like Nyanga [close to Cape Town]. The gut wrenching impact of squalor and day-to-day desperation to which many of our fellow South Africans are subjected, tends to put a test match at Newlands into perspective.*[22]

For an organisation like the South African Council of Sport (SACOS), which had adopted a position of doctrinal purity and had stayed outside the unification process, it was precisely the contrast between lush, well-manicured sporting fields in white areas, and the sheer struggle for survival in nearby dusty black townships, that added a grotesque dimension to the spectacle of establishment sport and vindicated their position of 'no normal sport in an abnormal society'. SACOS argued that sport played on this basis was not truly non-racial, that the unity that was achieved was a 'sham-unity', and that despite the political changes in the country, the existing social and political disparities were perpetuated in the new order. The reconstruction of South African society, and with it South African sport, was far more important than playing international sport for SACOS.[23]

Steve Tshwete adopted a more pragmatic view. He fully acknowledged the discrepancies, but nevertheless argued that sport could act as a 'healer' in a country torn by race, cultural and other differences. For this to happen, it was necessary to move away from the notion that rugby was mainly an Afrikaner game and soccer mainly a black game in South Africa.[24] Patel saw this as a long-term process. Although he had his reservations about some aspects of the development programme, he realised that a situation which had grown over years could not be turned about overnight. Nevertheless, he regarded the unification process as an important breakthrough which has ensured that 'SARFU belongs to the future children of South Africa'. It was therefore, he claimed, 'unreasonable' for those who had 'planted the tree of unification to expect to immediately reap the fruits of the tree'.[25]

As a result of adopting such flexible positions before the advent of majority rule, South Africa was readmitted to international sport. Whether the unification process and sport in general could add significantly to dissloving racial tensions and whether a game like rugby could realistically be expected to play a part in easing the burdens of those in the townships, remained a moot point. It is more likely that, given the institutional strength of 'white' rugby, and once the game is uncoupled from wider political concerns, the development programme may suffer correspondingly.

Not rugby as usual?

The first international rugby teams to visit South Africa after 1990 were the All Blacks from New Zealand, the traditional rivals of South African rugby; and the Wallabies from Australia, the World Cup champions at the time. These teams came out in August 1992. Although they visited the 'new' South Africa, many of the tensions of the old order remained unresolved. Before and during their visit the politics of transition often spilled over into the sporting arena.

It was with great anticipation that the South African rugby public awaited the contests with New Zealand and Australia. But not all rugby supporters realised that the tours were only able to take place because of political processes which were under way in the country and that the position adopted by the ANC was crucial in allowing international sport to take place. Some of the rugby fanatics in the *platteland* were therefore able to tell an Australian journalist: 'Ja … Mandela is a terrorist and must die', and in the same breath ask, 'but do you think Naas [Botha] is up to the All Black and Wallaby flyhalves?'[26]

While popular misconceptions and prejudices on the *platteland* and elsewhere were not likely to be dislodged by an appeal to reason, SARFU as the highest rugby authority in the land had to show itself supportive of the process which had made the tours possible in the first place. This necessitated a re-assessment of the significance of sporting symbols of an earlier era, such as rugby's supreme symbol – the Springbok.

With the establishment of a new rugby union and South African rugby on the brink of emerging from apartheid isolation, symbols of an earlier era were seen as inappropriate by some. Mluleki George, formerly of SARU and a committee member of the newly-formed SARFU, argued that the Springbok emblem represented the hurtful years of apartheid and white supremacy. In the new era, it had to be replaced by a more representative symbol. Such views caused an outcry amongst rugby traditionalists for whom South Africa's rugby history was intimately tied up with the Springbok emblem. Moreover, they did not regard the Springbok as a symbol of apartheid. It was officially approved as an emblem of the SARB in 1903 and first used on an overseas tour in 1906-1907, thus preceding the apartheid period under National Party rule. But white supremacy went back much further than the beginnings of National Party rule in 1948, and for the general public the Springbok was undoubtedly a sectional symbol, representing whites and predominantly Afrikaners. Before the arrival of the touring teams, a compromise was reached: the Springbok from the SARB was retained, but combined with four proteas and a rugby ball from SARU. After the World Cup of 1995, however, the Springbok emblem will be reviewed again.[27]

Rugby administrators not only had to come to an agreement on the Springbok emblem; they also had to adopt positions on the continuing violence in the country, which at one point threatened to scuttle the impending tours. In the two years between 1990 and the end of 1991, over six thousand had lost their lives in politically-motivated violence.[28] In general terms, a variety of pressures contributed to the violence: rapid urbanisation of black people once the earlier restrictions and restraints of apartheid had fallen away; growing class differentiation and competition over scarce resources; and intense political rivalry and jockeying, often assuming an outwardly ethnic form.[29] The question of violence had reached crisis proportions in mid-1992, especially after a particular vicious slaying in the township of Boipatong in the Vaal Triangle where 44 people, amongst them several women and children, were hacked to death. Although many South Africans had already become desensitised by continuing mayhem in the townships, the sheer brutality of these killings shocked anew. Allegations of a 'third force' and possible police complicity in the massacre at Boipatong compounded matters further. These tragic events dramatically underscored the need for the immediate termination of violence as a national priority agreed to by all.

In ANC quarters, it was strongly felt that it would have been insensitive for national sporting events to carry on as usual. Referring to Boipatong, Steve Tshwete argued that South Africans 'could not afford to behave as a normal nation, as if nothing has happened. The feeling is that we want to come together as South Africans during this period of mourning'.[30] Tshwete was also concerned about allegations that the police were connected to the violence; if that was the case, he argued, players from the police and security forces should be purged from top teams because they belonged in the camp of the 'enemy' and associated themselves with violence.[31]

Tshwete's assumptions about a common South African nationhood might have been premature and his views on the police and sport an oversimplification of more complex issues. But the ANC did not really need watertight arguments – they had more than sufficient political influence and leverage. As one commentator observed at the time: 'It is a simple fact that, currently, the ANC's huge standing overseas means no game can be played, no race run, no tour hosted without its approval'.[32] Rather than risking possible cancellation of the tours, SARFU negotiated with the ANC and came to an agreement that suitable respect would be shown at all test matches to the victims of violence.[33]

This, however, was not to be. On the day of the test against the All Blacks (15 August 1992), the crowd was in a defiant mood. They had their rugby back; the celebrated green and gold jerseyed Springboks were about to tackle the mighty All Blacks. It was an historic return to the international arena after years of isolation; an occasion brimful of nostalgia and tradition for predominantly Afrikaner male rugby fanatics who vividly recalled test matches which they had attended in the 'old' South Africa. It was not an occasion where they were going to comply meekly with ANC demands – an organisation which little more than two years previously they had regarded as a band of terrorists.

Large sections of the crowd were intent on ignoring the agreement between the ANC and SARFU that the National Anthem (*Die Stem*) would not be sung officially at the test, that the existing South African flag would not be hoisted, and that a minute's silence for those who had died at Boipatong would be observed. The ANC regarded this as a reasonable position and a reflection that the country had as yet no credible national symbols and that many were dying in the townships.[34] Such compromises might have saved the tour, but they also demonstrated a certain naivete. There was a vast gulf between seemingly rational boardroom decisions, and the behaviour of exuberant, if not inflamed, rugby supporters, convinced that the decisions were taken to humiliate them as a community.

Early on there were signs of trouble. Encouraged by the Afrikaans press, amongst other institutions, thousands of fans arrived with the national flag symbolising white South Africa at Ellis Park and plenty more were on sale at the stadium. This was unusual. For a crowd to make so much of the national flag at test matches had never been part of South African rugby culture or tradition. Spectators had not previously shown any real interest in the flag. But now, as the crowd wished to make a political point in an orchestrated fashion, the popularity of the flag soared to unprecedented heights. To discern the political message was not difficult as some inebriated fans waved their flags and chanted in unison: '*F... die ANC, f... die ANC*'. Inside the stadium notes were being passed around, urging the crowd to sing *Die Stem*, come what may.[35]

The showdown came when, just before the main game, the crowd was asked for a few moments' silence. Immediately close on 70 000 white people responded with a heartfelt rendition of *Die Stem*. One observer vividly recalled the occasion:

> *For that moment inside the concrete bowl, it seemed like a besieged tribe had gathered to take strength in their numbers and to send a message of defiance to their perceived persecutors. It felt like being in a bull-ring, and it was not certain whose blood was more passionately desired:*

that of the foe on the field or of the millions outside who
knew nothing of the ancient ritual but were believed to be
threatening it.[36]

What added to this defiant performance was that the anthem, contrary to the previous agreement, but with the blessing of Louis Luyt from SARFU, was played on the public address system. On the field South Africa did rather well, losing only by a narrow margin, but off the field the behaviour of the crowd elicited strong negative opinion. Black commentators regarded the singing of *Die Stem* – an anthem closely associated with apartheid – as deliberately provocative and the very antithesis of the spirit of change. Tshwete also came under fire for allowing himself, or so it seemed, to be used by the white rugby community:

White South Africa thanked him in a very special way ... the
way only white South Africa can ... They cocked their snook
at him and made it plain that now he had marvelously
played his part of the useful idiot, he should kindly
'voertsek' [clear off] and leave them to their 'traditional
ways of life' and pastimes. Poor man.[37]

Tshwete himself said that given the agitation before the time, the display of the 'apartheid flag' was to be expected and there was little that could be done about it. But he was very annoyed that the minute's silence was not observed and that the anthem was being played officially:

The signal they wanted to send was 'to hell with the blacks
and Boipatong'. It was a refusal, with contempt, to identify
with the plight of their compatriots who are on the receiving
end of violence.[38]

For a while the real possibility existed that the following week's test against the Wallabies at Newlands, Cape Town, would be cancelled. Australian Rugby Union president, Joe French, said that the team was ready to go home, should the ANC demand it. SARFU, however, apologised for the incident and distanced itself from the order to play *Die Stem*.[39] With this, the match was saved.

Symbolically the behaviour of the crowd can be seen as the last convulsions of a dying order – it was an act of nationalistic cultural defiance by people who knew that politically the South Africa they had known and supported had all but vanished. Almost in desperation they challenged the ANC, saying: 'Here is my anthem, here is my flag. Here I stand today and I sing: *"Ons sal lewe, ons sal sterwe! Ons vir jou Suid-Afrika!"* '[40] But emotionally gratifying as such a stance might have been, it had no wider political purchase because the world outside the stadium had changed irreversibly. It was also an one-off act; although a fair number of flags were in evidence at Newlands the following week, the minute's silence was observed and the crowd refrained from singing the national anthem *en masse*.[41] All in all it was a far less brazen display of Afrikaner nationalism at Newlands than at Ellis Park.

Currently, under a democratically elected government, the new South African flag – representing the spirit of the 'small miracle' of the country's relatively successful formal political transition – has made some headway amongst rugby supporters. Miniatures of the flag are also sewn onto the shorts of national team members. Whether the new flag will dominate against the old among South African spectators at the World Cup tournament remains to be seen.

The Luyt and World Cup shows

South African rugby lurched from crisis to crisis in the post-isolation period. On the field, despite a promising start against the All Blacks in August 1992, the Springboks had yet to win a series against the top rugby-playing countries after two years. The selectors kept on ringing the changes – a record number of players became Springboks – but found it difficult to find a winning combination.

Off the field, matters were not much better as various controversies dogged SARFU. Central to much of the drama was the larger-than-life Louis Luyt, president of SARFU in 1994. Luyt had succeeded Patel, the latter having taken over the reins after the death of long-serving rugby supremo, Danie Craven. Patel had declared himself unavailable for re-election in 1994 and this left the door open for Luyt to be elected unopposed as president. The circumstances surrounding Patel's resignation are not clear. He claimed that his work as headmaster of Lenasia Muslim School (close to Johannesburg) precluded further involvement with rugby, but whether this can be taken as a full explanation is open to question.

Further investigation into the political manoeuvering and machinations of different factions, which did not necessarily coincide with race, may shed more light upon this issue. At this point, however, it does appear that a number of board members did not regard Patel as suitable for the post of president. He was described as

an extremely ... nice-to-know person ... [but] has not in any
way proven – apart from his historical importance in so far
as unification is concerned – that he has the 'guts and
thunder' bona fides of what is expected from a national
rugby president.[42]

In Louis Luyt, SARFU certainly found a 'guts and thunder' president. At times he created the impression that he actively sought confrontation. 'You name it, Louis Luyt has fought over it', was the way one journalist summed it up:

Shamateurism, provincialism, provincial poaching, dinner
invitations, selection policies, team discipline, world cup
venues, the bad manners of other people, the absence of due
deference to his own eminence.[43]

Luyt's decision to allow *Die Stem* to be played at Ellis Park, his arguments with the International Rugby Board, and his unseemly public wrangles with Jannie Engelbrecht, Springbok manager of the 1994 tour to New Zealand, caused a considerable outcry. At one point, amidst the fight with Engelbrecht, Luyt even briefly resigned from the presidency. Luyt's track record and his tendency to ride roughshod over opponents called forth the unflattering comment that he was a man with 'less sensitivity and fewer principles than a rugby ball'.[44] His outbursts were also seen as damaging to the image of South

African rugby administration, giving the impression to the outside world that local administrators were 'a clamorous rat pack of barefoot yokels squabbling in the dust of a distant country'.[45]

Such criticisms need perspective. Luyt's background was not that of the usual solidly middle-class rugby administrator. His was a rags-to-riches story. Luyt was born in 1932 and went to school in the barren Karoo village of Hanover. During the depression years of the early 1930s, his father worked as a farm labourer, earning a paltry wage. As the son of a 'poor white', Luyt put himself through university at Bloemfontein. His first major business, a fertilizer company, Triomf, grew from humble beginnings as a one-man farm door-to-door selling operation into a multi-million rand concern. However, with the crash on the Johannesburg Stock Exchange in the 1980s, his company collapsed. Critics claimed that Luyt had taken his money out in advance, but he denies this. Be that as it may, Luyt as a businessman was far from finished. Currently he has a hand in several businesses; from his Cape farms alone he expects to earn R20 million in exports within three years. He also owns a private jet, and it is rumoured that on board the supersonic aircraft, surrounded by executive splendour, officials from the former non-establishment unions, not used to being entertained in such luxury, have been inclined to shift their political positions.

Not all of Luyt's enterprises were equally well-considered. In the late 1970s he was embroiled in a national scandal for acting as a front man in a government bid to run a sympathetic pro-apartheid newspaper with taxpayers' money. He claimed he was deliberately misled.[46]

In the world of rugby administration, Luyt's undoubted business acumen stood him in good stead. He turned losses incurred from the giant Ellis Park stadium into profits by adding 50 private suites for rental, and renting the stadium out for international soccer matches and other entertainment. He also raised the sponsorship of rugby in South Africa from R35-million to R85-million.[47] Although critics found it hard to fault his financial achievements, he was accused of running rugby affairs like a personal fiefdom, to the extent of involving close family members in arrangements for the World Cup. He responded by claiming that his family did not benefit financially from their involvement.[48]

For Luyt himself, there was a close connection between his aggressive style and the route that he had to travel to get to the top. 'I've tried to psycho-analyse myself', he said:

Why am I like I am? I think it's because I've always had to fight for myself. I had to fight for eight years before I went to varsity, and even then, I had to work at night to support myself. That could be the problem with my life. I had to fight for everything I ever got ... I wasn't a favourite. I wasn't a Broeder, didn't belong to any organisations. That's bullshit. I have always been my own master.[49]

At times Luyt's blunt, pragmatic and goal-orientated approach showed little appreciation for wider political matters. Hence, when rising levels of pre-election violence in 1994 threatened to derail plans for the World Cup, Luyt argued in racial terms that it was a 'black' and not a 'white' problem, and that as far as the World Cup was concerned, supporters could easily be isolated from what was going on in the rest of the country. 'Most of the violence has been outside Johannesburg', he said. 'It has been black-on-black violence, not black-on-white. We will certainly make sure that everybody visiting South Africa is booked into the right places.'[50]

Post-1990 politics in South Africa was even more of a minefield than before and Luyt, almost without fail, triggered several explosions. Along with the Ellis Park anthem debacle, he has gained a reputation in certain quarters 'as an archetypal worst of old-style white South Africans – brash and arrogant, proud of his lack of concern for his fellow citizens ...'[51]

It would be misleading, though, to view Luyt only in the light in which certain sections of the media have chosen to portray him. In a wider context, Luyt represents more than an abrasive and offensive personality. He symbolises the passing of an amateur 'gentlemen' era and the beginning of a new, more overtly professional, era with concomitant competitive management styles. The demands of the game have changed. Top players play an increasing number of first class games in each year, sometimes more than 40; and combined with practises, trials and training camps, this leaves them little time to pursue a career. At the same time stadiums have to show a profit by attracting spectators, and in a large measure this depends on winning games. This places players under additional strain. Given this situation Luyt, with his penchant for business, regards professionalism in rugby union as a logical development: 'We're using players to build mountains of cash and new stadia. They give ten years of their life to rugby and we have a duty to them.'[52] These sorts of views have brought him into conflict with the 'true blue amateurs' of the International Rugby Board (IRB), who had consistently, if not always convincingly, argued for the continuing amateur status of the game. Luyt has not only rejected their views on pay-rugby, but regards the tradition and ethos they stand for with disdain:

> *I saw the last World Cup in England and it was laughable. There is a great problem with the five unions ... They were fighting over who would wear World Cup blazers. They'd spent bloody hours discussing petty matters and who could go to dinners and who could sit nearest to the queen. It was all very petty.*[53]

Such forthright opinions were not designed to win friends – and they did not. SARFU was requested by the IRB to investigate Luyt's remarks as well as his views on professionalism in rugby. Perhaps not altogether surprising, an internal hearing cleared Luyt of charges that he was 'bringing the game into disrepute'. Luyt toned down his views of professionalism in rugby to the effect that he claims to believe in the amateur game, but that sufficient cognisance should be taken of the commercialisation of the sport.[54]

Luyt's general outlook was in marked contrast to that of Craven who, until the 'rebel' New Zealand tour of 1986, had felt very much at home amongst the luminaries of the rugby establishment and who was dead against professional rugby. In the cosy and clubbish world of the IRB, Craven had earned respect from his fellow administrators for being a 'most charming colleague, a good listener as well as a fine advocate, who was ... utterly committed to maintaining all that is best in the traditions of amateur rugby football.'[55] His stature in the United Kingdom, it was said, 'bordered on the awesome'.[56] True, like Luyt, Craven could also be autocratic, but his style and relations with the IRB were of a completely different order to those of Luyt. Craven could appreciate the almost old-world atmosphere that permeated the rugby establishment; for a brash businessman such as Luyt, the IRB was a relic of the past, reeking of decay and constituting an obstacle to more effective and progressive management. Confidently he could proclaim that, as far as organisation for the World Cup was concerned: 'We are up to date. We are waiting ... for the World Cup directors to catch up with us now. We've got everything under control. We do it professionally.'[57]

For SARFU it was of great importance to project South Africa as a suitable host country for staging the 1995 World Cup. For a while, though, there had been some doubt as to whether it should take place in South Africa at all. Keith Rowlands, secretary of the International Rugby Board, had his reservations because of the intermittent squabbling between SARFU and the ANC, and especially the high levels of political violence. Ultimately the staging of the World Cup in South Africa depended on politics; the country could boast excellent venues and a sound infrastructure; but without political stability, trouble-free rugby could not be guaranteed. The directors of the World Cup had only come to the decision in January 1993, once they had been given adequate assurances by the ANC and the government that South Africa's volatile politics would not affect the event. Even so the directors realised that a close watch had to be kept on the situation.[58]

As the fourth largest sporting event in the world, millions of rands are involved in organising the tournament. With the first World Cup in 1987, rugby union joined the worldwide trend towards increasingly commercialised sport. High-flying British advertising 'whizz kid', Patrick Nally, was instrumental in obtaining the sponsorships and advertising required for the launching of the first World Cup. Nally, who made his name and fortune in the world of sports management, has been described as a

fast-moving, fast-talking salesman with nothing more
tangible to peddle to major corporations than the idea that

sport could be a medium for communication, as sponsorship or advertising or just public relations.[59]

In a relatively short period, Nally was able to build up an impressive client list which included Ford Motor Company, Benson and Hedges cigarettes, Kraft Foods, Coca Cola, Canon, Seiko and Adidas. Linking up with the likes of Nally meant that rugby union, though officially still an amateur game, committed itself to a world where agents and advertisers turn fame into fortunes. Once this occurred, the game, the players and its administration could never be the same again.

In South Africa, an annual increase of 26 per cent in sport sponsorship between 1985 and 1992 also contributed to increased commercialisation.[60] As far as rugby is concerned, Luyt's thinly disguised support for increased professionalism has been noted. Amongst the players, South African rugby captain François Pienaar, has expressed the hope that rugby will become a professional sport after the World Cup in 1995.[61]

The process of greater commercialisation of the game in South Africa had its roots in the years of South Africa's isolation. In the absence of international competition, the country lacked a national rugby identity and the game revolved around the provincial Currie Cup competition and the need to fill stadiums for gain. Winning the Currie Cup became all important as it represented the pinnacle of what could be achieved nationally. The result was that financial incentives were used to lure star players across provincial boundaries.[62] The issue of payment for rugby was not, however, restricted to South Africa. Besides players from South Africa, Australians have regularly embarked on an off-season exodus to Italy and France, and it was not, as one official noted wryly, 'because they liked pasta or the language'.[63]

Although some rugby administrators in Britain had deep reservations about the way the game was moving, somewhat ironically the World Cup itself, which they supported, provided an additional impetus towards further commercialisation. Despite some initial hiccups, the 1991 World Cup generated a profit of R150-million for the organisers, and this did not take into account the multi-million rand spin-offs for local tourist operators. The 1995 World Cup has a target sponsorship of R170-million and one of its sponsors is the world's largest consumer payment system, Visa.[64]

With the World Cup, rugby union has become part of the world-wide entertainment industry and rugby players have become the entertainers. Given this situation, it is hardly surprising that pressures have started to mount for the players – who are, after all, central to the event – to receive fair financial reward for their efforts. Rugby union is evidently fast on its way to becoming a huge capitalist enterprise. There are strong indications that, in spite of opposition from England, amongst others, rugby-playing countries such as South Africa, Australia, France and possibly New Zealand may go fully professional after the World Cup.[65]

South Africa's re-entry into international sport after 1990 also involved an entry into the world of the international sports industry, and the World Cup rugby tournament will be the country's first experience of staging a sporting event of this scale and financial scope. Tourism, transport, hotels, game reserves, restaurants, enter-tainment, the liquor and soft drinks business and manufacturing (clothes, sports equipment and souvenirs) will all be looking to an increase in profits from the tournament. An influx of thousands of foreigners is expected and a mini tourist boom is predicted:

> *Lured by the prospect of five weeks of thrilling rugby (as a
> live and television spectacle the tournament has few peers in
> the sporting world today) to add to the conventional
> attractions the Republic has to offer, like sun, golden
> beaches, unsurpassed game reserves and glorious climate,
> they will arrive from New Zealand, Australia, Britain,
> France, Japan, Canada, the United States and South
> America. And they'll spend money like water. The hugely
> favourable – for overseas tourists clutching dollars, pounds
> and yen – exchange rate means fans will be able to stay at a
> leading hotel for four nights at the cost of a single night in
> the United Kingdom.*[66]

It remains to be seen whether such optimistic expectations will be fully realised.

The significance of the World Cup for wider South African society is debatable. Apart from the much vaunted status and prestige of being able to host the competition, it has to be recognised that the World Cup is essentially a 'first world' event, increasingly being driven by international capital. The super-spectacle will, in the first place, be geared towards the more affluent. Tickets for the major games, if obtainable, are far beyond the reach of many ordinary white South Africans, not to mention township dwellers if they happen to be interested.

It has been reported that the World Cup organisers had pledged R100 000 towards the development of rugby – an amount which Tshwete has slammed as 'frivolous'. He expects the 'big unions to make significant contributions to our communities'.[67] But even if these contributions are increased considerably, it will still not disguise the fact that structurally the World Cup and its concerns are heavily weighted in favour of a minority of elites in the country. While the substantial economic multiplier effect from the World Cup may produce sorely- needed employment opportunities, too much should not be read into this: the World Cup injection into the local economy is likely, in most cases, to have a temporary effect only.

Sporting events like the World Cup in a divided society such as South Africa are often justified in terms of sport as a 'great healer'. This notion, however laudable, contains a number of questionable assumptions. But even if its basic premise is accepted, it still remains a pre-condition that sportspeople should be able to meet as equals across the racial and class divides for sport to have any chance of working its supposed 'healing magic'. With its capitalist dynamic and geared, as it is, towards a certain elite section of the society, the World Cup does not appear to meet this fundamental pre-condition. The organisers, administrators, players, spectators and television viewers will be largely restricted to the upper classes in South Africa and their counterparts in 'first world' countries. Given this, it is unlikely that the World Cup can act as a bridge to the masses and help soften social divisions.

It has been said of the Olympic Games that 'by organising the sports spectacle, capital puts over its most extravagant image throughout a world in which whole populations suffer from illiteracy, famine and poverty'.[68] Is there reason to believe that the 1995 Rugby World Cup will be any different?

Notes

1. *Die Burger*, 5 February 1990 (translation).
2. *Rugby 15*, May 1990.
3. *Die Burger*, 5 February 1990 (translation).
4. *City Press*, 2 December 1990.
5. *Sunday Star*, 18 February 1990.
6. *New Nation*, 8 November 1990.
7. T. Lodge, 'The African National Congress in the 1990s' in G. Moss and I. Obery (eds), *South African Review 6: From 'Red' Friday to Codesa* (Johannesburg 1992) p. 70.
8. *Business Day*, 28 January 1991.
9. *New Nation*, 8 November 1990.
10. *Weekly Mail*, 8 March 1991.
11. Compare *Sunday Times*, 27 January 1991.
12. *Pretoria News*, 9 December 1991; *Die Burger*, 15 February 1992; P. Dobson, *Doc: The life of Danie Craven* (Cape Town 1994) pp. 182, 187.
13. *Beeld*, 6 April 1989.
14. *Rapport*, 19 July 1992 (translation). See also *Die Volksblad*, 13 July 1992.
15. *Eastern Province Herald*, 18 July 1994; *Eastern Province Herald*, 22 July 1994; *Die Burger*, 21 July 1992.
16. *The Star*, 16 August 1994.
17. *Rugby 15*, October/November 1993.
18. *The Argus*, 3 June 1994; *Sunday Times*, 7 January 1994.
19. *Sunday Times*, 16 August 1992.
20. *Rugby 15*, October/November 1993.
21. Compare *Die Burger*, 12 June 1992; *Die Volksblad*, 30 May 1994.
22. *Sunday Star*, 23 August 1992.
23. *City Press*, 7 June 1992.
24. *Weekend Argus*, 5 March 1994.
25. *Rugby 15*, August 1993. See also *Weekly Mail and Guardian*, 13 May 1993.
26. *Weekly Mail and Guardian*, 13 August 1992.
27. Compare *Evening Post*, 15 June 1992; *Die Burger*, 22 June 1992; *Die Volksblad*, 27 July 1992; *Rugby 15*, September 1993; *Beeld*, 4 June 1994.
28. South African Institute of Race Relations, *Race Relations Survey, 1991/92* (Johannesburg 1992) p. lxiii.
29. M. Morris and D. Hindson, 'The disintegration of apartheid: from violence to reconstruction' in Moss and Obery (eds), *South African Review 6* p. 157.
30. *Pretoria News*, 24 June 1992.
31. *The Star*, 23 June 1992.
32. *Sunday Times*, 5 July 1992.
33. *Beeld*, 10 July 1992.
34. *Weekly Mail and Guardian*, 27 August 1994.
35. *The Star*, 17 August 1994.

36.   *The Star*, 17 August 1994.
37.   *The Sunday Star*, 23 August 1992.
38.   *The Star*, 22 August 1992.
39.   *Sowetan*, 18 August 1992.
40.   *Beeld*, 17 August 1992 (translation). See also *Rapport*, 16 August 1992.
41.   *Cape Times*, 24 August 1992; *Business Day*, 24 August 1992.
42.   *Rugby 15*, April 1994.
43.   *The Star*, 19 August 1994.
44.   *Weekly Mail and Guardian*, 27 August 1992.
45.   *Weekly Mail and Guardian*, 25 August 1994.
46.   *The Star*, 19 August 1994; *Natal on Saturday*, 27 August 1994; *Sowetan*, 18 July 1992; personal communication.
47.   *Rugby 15*, July 1993; *The Sunday Star*, 12 July 1992; *Weekly Mail and Guardian*, 12 August 1994.
48.   *Beeld*, November 1994.
49.   *The Star*, 19 August 1994.
50.   *The Citizen*, 31 March 1994.
51.   *Weekly Mail and Guardian*, 27 August 1992.
52.   *The Star*, 19 August 1994. See also *Cape Times*, 4 November 1994.
53.   *Sunday Times*, 23 October 1994.
54.   *Pretoria News*, 12 November 1994.
55.   B. Booyens, *Danie Craven* (Cape Town 1975) p. 189.
56.   *Cape Times*, 26 August 1994.
57.   *Rugby 15*, September 1994.
58.   *Cape Times*, 20 January 1993.
59.   N. Wilson, *The Sports Business* (London 1988) p. 177.
60.   *Finansies en Tegniek*, 7 August 1992.
61.   *Die Volksblad*, 25 June 1994.
62.   *Rugby News*, September 1994; *Natal on Saturday*, 16 July 1994.
63.   *Natal on Saturday*, 16 July 1994.
64.   *Cape Times*, 22 January 1993; *Beeld*, 4 November 1994; *Pretoria News*, 5 November 1994.
65.   *Metro*, 11 November 1994; *Rugby News*, September 1994.
66.   *The Star*, 22 January 1993.
67.   *Sowetan*, 29 April 1994.
68.   J-M. Brohm, *Sport: A prison of measured time* (London 1989) p. 173.

CHAPTER TWO

'The thing that is not round'

The untold story of black rugby in South Africa*

André Odendaal

Recently retired South African rugby legend Uli Schmidt was known throughout the rugby playing world as a brilliant, bruising hooker with a penchant for popping up in the most unexpected places to score tries. But off the field he continues to play according to old rules. In 1994 he declared that rugby was not a natural game for blacks to play. 'It is not in their culture', he said. 'They should play soccer'.[1] Schmidt was echoing what most white rugby players in South Africa have come to accept as truth. And although they try to cloak this fact in new-South-Africa-speak, their views are grounded in old-style apartheid ideology, which implicitly explains racial domination and discrimination as 'natural'.

As late as 1977 the official South African Year Book claimed that

> it is only comparatively recently that the Black peoples have
> shown a marked increase in what may be called modern
> sporting activities. For centuries they found their recreation
> in traditional activities, such as hunting and tribal dances. It
> was the White nation, with its European background and
> tradition, which participated in the recognised sports ...[2]

Past Springbok captains transmitted this apartheid thinking in almost unabridged form. In 1971 Hannes Marais, now convenor of the South

African selection panel, suggested that: 'The Coloured population does not seem very interested in sport. They do not play much rugby and cricket'.[3] In 1980 Dawie de Villiers, now a cabinet minister in Nelson Mandela's government of national unity, declared: 'Don't forget that the Blacks have really known western sports [only] for the last ten years. [Therefore] they have naturally not yet reached the same standard'.[4]

The time has come to bury the myth that current inequalities in rugby evolved naturally; that they existed because black South Africans were not interested in the game or were not suited to it, psychologically, emotionally and physically. This underlying assumption, which still directly and indirectly permeates the game despite rugby 'unity' and the achievement of political democracy, is one of the main reasons for the muddled arrogance and unhappiness that has characterised South African rugby in recent years. The fact that it is still articulated with such smugness is an example of a deep-seated and enduring racism in South African sport and society. For the future of the game, racism in its overt as well as hidden forms needs to be addressed at the highest levels by rugby administrations.

Black rugby players and sportspeople are relatively underdeveloped as a direct result of South Africa's history of colonialism, segregation and apartheid. Sport in South Africa has always been linked closely to politics and has reflected the society and social structures. This can be seen on various levels: in the organisational structures that developed, in the value systems that became entrenched in sport, in the issues that excited sportspeople over the years, in the differences that emerged amongst them, and in the way the development of sport closely followed the pattern of historical and regional development.

Contrary to general knowledge, black South Africans have a long, indeed remarkable, rugby and sporting history. This piece is the first work that locates black rugby firmly in an historical context, identifies the main contours of its development and analyses internal problems and contradictions, while also providing some details of general interest for rugby followers. It has drawn largely from, and tries to build on, three important earlier works. Firstly, the labour of love by the late Braber Ngozi, a star rugby player from the 1930s and 1940s, who made it his life's task to collect brochures, news reports and personal reminiscences on the history of black rugby.[5] Secondly, the 1981 academic article by Jeff Peires which started exploring the history of African rugby in the Eastern Cape and helped bring the importance of sport in understanding South African history to the notice of academic researchers.[6] And, finally, the chapters on black rugby by Paul Dobson, official historian of the old establishment South African Rugby Board.

Although this chapter cannot provide the definitive history of black rugby, it assists in recovering and understanding a story that has been scandalously ignored, to the detriment of sport in South Africa.

Cape Town origins

Cape Town was the birthplace of South African sport as we know it today. After the British took over the Cape on a permanent basis early in the 19th century, soldiers and settlers introduced games like horse racing, cricket and, later on, rugby. For the British colonisers in the African and Asian colonies these sports and the clubs that were set up later served as symbols, not only of social, but also of political domination. As one historian has pointed out,

> *[the club] was developed as an enclave of power and privilege in an alien setting, its members patently different from the unadmitted millions not only in colour and status, but also in place. More than anywhere else it was the place where the imperialists celebrated their Britishness, authority and imperial lifestyle'.*[7]

Nevertheless, the local people, both black and white, soon came into contact with these sports, and starting giving them a distinct South African character. The historian Hattersley tells, for instance, of a horse race in Green Point, Cape Town, as early as the 1820s where '... Malays and Negroes mingled with whites, all crowding and elbowing, eager to get a sight of the momentous event'. One of the earliest artist's sketches of a rugby match in Cape Town also features spectators wearing the distinctive *koufeia* identified with the Cape

Muslim community. By the 1860s young men with names like Loben-
gula and Moshesh were playing cricket for Zonnebloem College, the
school started in District Six by Cape Governor Grey with the specific
aim of acculturating or 'civilising' the sons of African chiefs.[8]

Organised sport was still in its infancy at that stage. By the 1870s
there were only a few clubs in existence in larger centres like Cape
Town, Pietermaritzburg and Port Elizabeth, where sizeable numbers
of British soldiers, administrators and settlers could be found. Among
these was the first African cricket club started in Port Elizabeth in
1869.[9] No regional or national sports associations had been formed
and there were no official leagues or competitions. It was only
between 1875 and 1885 that sport became institutionalised. In those
ten years the first rugby, soccer, athletics, cycling, horse racing, golf
and tennis clubs were formed, and regular competitions were started.
From the 1880s onwards, national organisations were formed to place
sport on an organised footing.[10]

There were two main reasons for this growth in sport. The first
was the discovery of the richest mineral deposits in the world which
dramatically transformed South African life. Diamonds and gold
attracted large numbers of European fortune seekers into the interior,
gave rise to industries and towns, and encouraged Britain to extend
its sphere of power. This led to the so-called Anglo-Boer War and the
new Union of South Africa which, in 1910, drew previously frag-
mented political territories into a single state. Secondly, during the
last half of the 19th century sport became a mass leisure activity
catering for the large populations moving to the new urban environments which sprang up following the Industrial Revolution in Britain.
Within South Africa, new arrivals from Britain started emulating what
was happening at 'home'.

When the British colonists started to form clubs, competitions and
regional and national organisations, black sportspeople soon followed
suit, particularly in Cape Town, the Eastern Province and Kimberley.
The Western Province Coloured Rugby Union (WPCRU), for
example, was formed in Cape Town in 1886, only three years after
white rugby players had formed their own exclusive Western Province Rugby Football Union. The founding clubs of the WPCRU were
Roslyns from District Six, Violets from Claremont, Good Hopes and

Arabian College from the Bo-Kaap (or what was then commonly known as the Malay Quarter). Later these clubs were joined by Hamediahs, founded in 1896, and other teams. In 1898 competition was put on a formal footing with the Fernwood Cup competition for first division teams in the union.[11]

As the names Arabian College and Hamediahs indicate, the teams in the Fernwood Cup were drawn from the cohesive and well-established Muslim community in Cape Town. Although the Cape Muslims became passionate rugby and cricket followers at an early stage, they adopted the new games on their own terms, giving them a distinctive character and meaning. The values of muscular Christianity and the British empire attached to sport by the ruling classes and the church schools of the time obviously did not have the same relevance for Muslim sportspeople.

Teams were community based, often coming from one street, a family group or the 'Jamaahs', organised groups meeting for religious purposes which spread out into the social sphere. Formal sports clubs emerged from these communal activities.[12] The teams were predominantly Muslim. A local Muslim sports historian has explained why this was so:

> They ... decided ... to organise on ethical and cultural
> grounds in order to keep the Muslims of the Cape together
> and also to bring unity amongst them. As most of the leading
> administrators were also the Imams of the congregation,
> they felt it was better to organise separately as they were
> mostly against the drinking habits of the other groups,
> especially over the festive season.[13]

The local 'Malays', as the Muslims were generically (and often incorrectly) labelled, became colourful features of the white-only establishment rugby scene. Easily distinguished by their *koufeias* (or fezzes) and *liedjies* (songs), they became passionate supporters of local white clubs and the provincial team:

> The teams which had most support were near the people's
> homes – Varsity, Villagers and Hamiltons, and this led to

28

> *increased rivalry between the people of the city and those*
> *agter die Tol – beyond the Tollgate at Woodstock. These*
> *were above all the people of Claremont, known to the people*
> *of the city as Tamaleitjiedorp. If Villagers lost they would*
> *say, 'Die ligte is uit [the lights are out] in Tamaleitjiedorp'.*
> *And if Hamiltons lost ... the Malays of Claremont ... would*
> *say with delight, 'Vanaand is daar martial law in die Kaap'*
> *(tonight there is martial law in the Cape].*[14]

The Muslim supporters became synonymous too with the historic Newlands rugby ground. They were accommodated behind the posts in the segregated south stand (or Malay Stand) sitting in 'rows of red fezzes above smart grey suits'. For more than 30 years – from 1919 to 1953 – the legendary Gasant Ederoos Behardien (commonly known as Gamat) was the 'ballboy' for Western Province and South African teams. According to Paul Dobson, Gamat would inevitably appear at the tunnel 'elegant in his long white coat and red fez' to stir up a 'delicious prematch excitement'. *Doekums* or 'Malay tricks' meant to jinx the opposition and ward of bad luck for the home team became part of the Newlands folklore. Famous players like Bennie Osler, who carried a bag of *doepa* around with him on the 1931- 32 tour to Britain, (and was injured in the one match he failed to do so), were known to engage in superstitious rituals attributed to Muslim custom.

Osler was reputed to have been very close to the Muslim community, regularly coaching local teams and even helping to establish the Cape Malay Choir Board. One observer has pointed out that he was also a representative for the United Tobacco Company and that part of his duties were to be at local meetings to get players to use UTC products. Gamat the subservient jester and Osler the famous benefactor were reflections, from different ends of the spectrum, of the unequal and paternalistic relations that characterised sporting contacts between black and white at the Cape. White players sometimes helped coach black teams, or allowed them to use their fields, and the affinity which developed between the white rugby establishment at the Cape and the so-called Malay constituency was not paralleled anywhere else in South Africa. However, these contacts certainly did not challenge the racial order.

As a result of cultural and religious particularism, re-inforced by the segregationist politics of the state, not one, but several 'provincial' rugby boards eventually emerged from the black communities of Cape Town. This had a major impact on the history of black/non-racial rugby, complicating relations and leading to long-running tensions which spilled over at both local and national level.

Following the formation of the predominantly Muslim board in 1886, a second regional organisation, the City and Suburban Union, was formed in 1898. 'Cities' was based in Mowbray and its main club was Wanderers. Formed in 1886, it had won the championship 13 times by 1920, overshadowing rivals like Oaks, Thistles, Perserverance, Temperance and Californians. A correspondent reported in 1914 that the city and Suburban Union had impressive facilities, including a stand which could accommodate between 600 to 700 people, good dressing rooms, first-aid facilities and a 'nicely-kept refreshment stall' run by a 'very obliging lady and her daughter' who served cake and tea.[15]

The names of the early officials – Carelse, Maneveld and Mulder – confirm that this was a union representing a different sector of the black community. Club names like Temperance, Progress and Perserverance might have come straight out of John Bunyan's Pilgims Progress, as Dobson has indicated, and they showed how the contemporary values of Christianity and Victorian 'progress' had been internalised by sections of the black population. City and Suburban remained very specific about membership: as late as the 1960s a clause in its constitution forbade membership to Muslims.[16]

This kind of sectionalism existed in other sports as well, and remained a perennial problem in sport in Cape Town. For a time the Cape District Football Association did not admit Muslim clubs. Richard van der Ross claims that the reason for this was that the administrators of the separate Western Province Muslim Soccer League actually asked Cape District to exclude Muslim clubs 'in order to strengthen their own League'.[17] But this was only part of a complex story in which communities discriminated against on the basis of their colour developed their own internal hierarchies and sets of discriminatory values. As the legendary sports administrator, Hassan Howa, recalled:

> When I started playing cricket I found a very sad set up.
> Muslims played in one league, Christians in another,
> Indians in another. I couldn't fit in with the Malays, nor with
> the Indians and so I fell in with the Coloureds of the
> Wynberg Cricket Union ... conditions were highly
> discriminatory. One had to be a Christian before one could
> play for Western Province, one had to be a certain lightness
> and one had to be able to run a pencil through one's hair. It
> was then that I learnt to fight the whole reactionary
> establishment.[18]

Perserverance rugby club was among those which attached special importance to the lightness of one's skin. When the non-racial sports movement emerged in the 1950s it tried to counter these long-standing divisions amongst black sportspeople, but the old fault lines continued to open up from time to time – and even today their topography is still visible.

Meanwhile, by the turn of the century rugby had spread beyond the city of Cape Town to Stellenbosch, Paarl and other outlying areas. For example, the Central Rugby Football Union (Coloured) was in 1912 organising leagues involving Swellendam, Robertson, Heidelberg, Riversdale, Ladismith and Mossel Bay.[19] Statistics provided by Dobson show that by 1930 there were more than 200 black rugby clubs in Cape Town and the surrounding areas.[20] These included African rugby clubs, as we shall see below. Small wonder then that the Western Cape became the stronghold of black/non-racial rugby in South Africa. The sportspeople here were part of a long tradition. As city dwellers they were relatively affluent. They took part in large numbers. And they had closer connections with white establishment sport than anywhere else in the country.

The Eastern Cape as a cradle of rugby

The other important cradle of black sport in South Africa was the Eastern Cape. Here, dynamics very different to those in the relatively cosmopolitan Western Cape shaped the development of games like rugby and cricket. This region was the home of hundreds of thousands of Africans brought under British rule during the 19th century as Xhosa chiefdoms were conquered and incorporated into the expanding Cape Colony. British rule had a disruptive effect on the conquered societies. A European system of administration was imposed over them and agents of imperialism such as missionaries, teachers, traders and farmers moved into the African territories bringing the indigenous people into contact with alien European ideas and institutions. The missionaries, for example, set up schools and encouraged the people to forego their 'uncivilised' customs and obtain a Western education, learn about Christianity and adopt British cultural values. This led to the emergence of a market, rather than subsistence, oriented peasantry and a new class of literate, missionary-educated 'school' people. These people – teachers, ministers, law agents, clerks, interpreters, storemen, transport riders, blacksmiths, telegraph operators and printers – entertained high hopes that having accepted the way of the white man they would eventually be assimilated fully into the evolving Cape colonial society.

The Cape Colony constitution of 1853 provided for a qualified franchise which allowed all citizens, regardless of colour, to vote if they owned property to the value of £25 and could sign their names. By the mid-1880s around ten thousand Africans had registered as voters. They formed their own political organisations based on the example of the white political parties, started a newspaper and were so strong in some constituencies that they were able to return candidates of their choice to parliament.[21]

Sport was integral to this whole process of assimilation and mobilisation. Together with politics, education and religion, it was one of the many aspects of British culture that the new African elite enthusiastically adopted in pursuit of its assimilationist goals.

The mission schools, often racially mixed and providing education based on the English model, were the training grounds for black sportsmen. The numbers of people attending these schools rose from

2 827 pupils in 1865 to 15 568 pupils in about 700 schools by 1885. Recreation was a matter of supreme importance at these institutions as many of the cultural activities of tribal Africans were deemed 'incompatible with Christian purity of life' and had to be abandoned by those embracing the new religious ideas of the missionaries. Provision was, therefore, made for the 'profitable employment of leisure'.[22] Drill became a regular feature on time-tables and sports were introduced. Instructive of the relationship between religion, education, culture and sport was a report in a missionary newspaper of festivities in 1870 to celebrate the founding of one of the earliest African Sunday School unions. After a day-and-a-half of church services and festivities, the 700 young people involved 'broke up into parties for various sports'.[23] And on the Queen's birthday in 1877, all the pupils at Lovedale had a day of sport in the fields.[24]

If the schools were where Africans in the Eastern Cape were introduced to sport, they needed no encouragement to develop their interest after leaving these institutions. The first African-controlled newspaper, Imvo Zabantsundu (Native Opinion) – started in 1884 and still publishing today – abounded with copy of sport. These were printed under the heading of *Ibala labadlali* (sports reports), and by 1887 the newspaper had a 'sporting editor'. The big Dyer and Dyer merchant house placed advertisements in the newspaper directed specifically at African sportsmen and clubs.[25]

Cricket was by far the most popular sport. For the Victorians it embodied 'a perfect system of ethics and morals', and the school people of the Eastern Cape made it their own as well. By the mid-1880s there were thriving African cricket clubs and regular competitions in almost all areas in the region. Following the white precedent of the inter-town tournament for the Champion Bat, the precursor to the Currie Cup provincial competition, black cricketers started their own inter-town tournament in 1884. In a subsequent challenge match, the champions from King Williams Town beat their white counterparts who had taken part in the Champion Bat tournament. The Port Elizabeth Telegraph was not exaggerating when it observed that cricket 'seems quite to hit the Kaffir fancy'.[26]

After cricket, rugby, football and tennis were the next most popular games for the aspiring black petty bourgeoisie. Although rugby, or *mboxo* (the thing that is not round), was relatively slow in taking root in the region, it established itself in an enduring manner. Today the Eastern Province is virtually the only place in the country where rugby has a popularity rivalling soccer amongst Africans. The first black teams were probably institutional, based at Lovedale, Healdtown and the Kaffir Institution. Located in Grahamstown and run by the Anglican Church, the latter was a sister school to the white St Andrews College, which started playing the game as early as 1878. And, according to tradition, it was the St Andrews headmaster, Reverend Mullins, who introduced rugby to the black community.[27]

The first adult club in the region was Union Rugby Football which was formed in Port Elizabeth in 1887. According to records collected by rugby historian Braber Ngozi, the club was started by 'kitchen boys who learnt their rugby from whites'.[28] This could only have been part of the story because the first president, Stephen Katta, was one of the leading figures in the local Native Vigilance Committee through which the local elite of voters (totalling 274 in 1891), ministers and educated people represented African opinion in the town.[29] The headquarters of the club were at KwaMpundu, the present Mill Park, and the games were played at Dubula, where the provincial hospital now stands. At first Union's opponents were local coloured teams, which formed themselves into a Port Elizabeth Coloured Rugby Union in 1892; but in 1894 a second African club, Orientals, was formed, followed by the Morning Star, Rovers, Frontier and, in 1906, Spring Rose clubs.

Union and Orientals became the strongest teams, and their matches were modelled on the rivalry between the main white clubs, Crusaders and Olympics.

Around the turn of the century, the first major attempts at urban segregation occurred in the main towns of the Cape Colony. Following a pattern that would become familiar in South Africa during the 20th century, just over twenty thousand Africans from Port Elizabeth were pushed to the edges of the town, into new 'locations' at Korsten and New Brighton. Orientals became the Korsten club and Spring Rose, named after the area near Bedford from which most of its members had come, belonged to New Brighton, though the club's meetings continued to be held 'in the open air' in town.[30]

Contests between different towns in the Eastern Cape were taking place well before the turn of the century. Sometimes challenges would take place via the press, as when Grahamstown challenged towns like East London and King Williams Town in the columns of the *Imvo Zabantsundu* in 1899: '*Velani makwedini ase ma X[h]oseni*' (come on/show yourselves young boys of Xhosaland), the Grahamstown correspondent teased.[31] By 1904 the level of organisation and enthusiasm had reached the stage where the first inter-town tournament could be organised in Port Elizabeth. Teams from Grahamstown and East London participated.

Following on this event, an Eastern Province Native Rugby Union was formed in 1905. The first EPNRU president was Tobias Mvula and the secretary was R.R. Booi, an employee of the Union Castle shipping company. The inter-town fixtures were continued under the new union, and were played over a period of several weeks. After first round play-offs in the various localities, the winning local teams went on to play against other towns in the second round, leading to a final in Port Elizabeth for the Wynne's Cup, which had been presented by a local businessman. In 1906 there were nine teams playing for the Wynne's Cup: the 1905 champions Oriental, Union and Rovers (all Port Elizabeth), Zebras Football Club (Uitenhage), Lions Football Club (Cradock), and Wanderers, Winter Rose, Lilly White and Eastern Province Football Club (Grahamstown). The following year, they were joined by the Tigers club from Somerset East.[32] Founded in 1895, Tigers acquired their first jerseys after the South African War and chose the colours of the Union Jack – red, white and blue – 'in honour of the victors'. Up until 1926, when lorry transport was provided, the players of the club used to do a round trip of 80 kilometres by foot to fulfil fixtures against the neighbouring town of Cookhouse.[33]

The aim of the Eastern Province Native Rugby Union was clearly regional, but it does not seem to have been able to cover the whole of the vast area now formally called the Eastern Province. For example, in 1908 the Queenstown-based Winter Rose Rugby Football Club, which was not a member of the EPNRU, played no less than eight games, indicating that there were a number of rugby networks operating in the region.[34] Later, various other 'provincial' units based in East London, Queenstown, Aliwal North and Alice would emerge.

Meanwhile, coloured rugby players were playing in separate competitions. By 1912 there was a smoothly functioning Eastern Province Coloured Rugby Football Union based in Port Elizabeth. The two champion teams, which met in the final played at the prestigious St George's Park ground, were West End and the predominantly Muslim Red Crescent club. In the same year the EPCRFU combined with the EP Coloured Cricket Board to organise a special dance in the Town Hall to raise funds for the widows and children of local fishermen who had lost their lives in a fishing disaster. Clearly the Eastern Cape rugby players were respected members of their local communities, closely tied to what was happening there – and they were not without means, as the EPCRFU's credit balance of £25.12.4d in 1913 indicated.[35] But, here too, we see early patterns of segregation, which would be re-inforced by legislative decree and lived experience in later years.

The game goes national

Soon the game of rugby was spreading out from the cradles of black sport in Cape Town and what today constitutes the Eastern Province to other parts of the country. Artisans and school people from Cape Town and the Eastern Cape were among the hundreds of thousands of people who converged on the new mining centres in the late 19th century, or started working on the developing infrastructure unfolding magnetically northwards towards Kimberley and the Witwatersrand. Trained to participate in the colonial economy, they generally occupied the most sought after and best paid jobs available to black people: clerks, interpreters, teachers, ministers, etc. In the new cosmopolitan surroundings, they also started assuming positions of social prominence and began to imitate the middle class games and manners of the white ruling classes. Amongst other things, they started new choral, church, mutual improvement and sports associations.

Kimberley in particular became a cultural melting pot and a growth point for sport.[36] Here the Cape Town and Eastern Cape traditions described above became more closely intertwined than anywhere else. The different sectors of the black community and people from different religions played and organised together. A Griqualand West Colonial Rugby Football Union, consisting of coloured, 'Malay' (Moslem) and African clubs, was started in 1894. The four founding clubs – Universals, Violets (perhaps named after the Cape Town club), Excelsior from Beaconsfield and the Native Rovers Rugby Football Club – were soon joined by Progress and others. A correspondent from Kimberley proudly reported in *Imvo Zabantsundu* that the *amadodana* (young men) there were doing good work and that they had organised a trophy which could be seen in the window of Harris and Co. in the town. He challenged other areas to become organised as well.[37] The Union was soon running three divisions, the bottom one being for 'young men who are under 17'.[38] By the mid-1890s Kimberley also had three African tennis clubs – Blue Flag, Champion and Come Again – and a regional cricket association with no less than ten Indian, 'Malay', coloured and African teams.[39]

The Griqualand West Colonial Rugby Football Union (GWCRFU) was one of the very first sports organisations in South Africa which was specifically non-racial. In the Xhosa columns of *Imvo Zabantsundu* it was noted that it did not discriminate on the basis of '*bala, luhhlanga, lulwimi, nalunqulo*' (colour, nationality, language and religion).[40] This is the earliest evidence of this development thus far found. And the fact that the founders used 'colonial' in the name rather than the usual racial appellation to distinguish them from the white establishment body indicates that they were serious in their aims.

The secretary of the GWCRFU was the 25 year-old Isaiah Bud Mbelle. He was typical of the new generation of educated intellectuals and sports leaders. Educated at Healdtown, he taught first before becoming the first African to pass the qualifying examination for the Cape Civil Service. A speaker of no less than six languages, he was appointed as Interpreter in Native Languages to the Northern Circuit of the Supreme Court in Kimberley. His salary of £25 per month reputedly made him the highest paid African government employee in the colony.[41] Mbelle's sister later married Sol Plaatje, the famous journalist, writer and political figure. Their marriage accross traditional ethnic lines, which caused unhappiness in family circles, was yet another example of how the younger generation of western-educated, urbanised and Christianised intellectuals was crossing old boundaries and shaping new directions.

Clearly determined to emulate the example of white rugby players who had formed the whites-only South African Rugby Board in 1889 with its Currie Cup tournament (as well as the black cricketers who had by then organised various inter-town tournaments), the well-connected Bud Mbelle and his fellow rugby administrators in Kimberley initiated plans to start a national black rugby body and competitions. In 1897 they persuaded Cecil John Rhodes, the arch imperialist and symbol of the town's new wealth, to present 'all the Coloured Sporting People of South Africa with a Silver Cup, valued at Fifty Guineas, for Competition amongst themselves on the same lines as the Currie Cup'.[42]

The GWCRFU sent out a notice calling on clubs and 'Unions (if any)' in 'the various towns and districts' to send delegates to a meeting at the Savona Cafe in Kimberley on 19 August 1897. The aim was to form a South African Coloured Rugby Football Board (SACRFB).[43] The meeting was held one day after a team representing the GWCRFU left for a tournament in Cape Town where they were due to play seven matches. The turnout was disappointing. Only local people attended, although Bud Mbelle was requested by the Port Elizabeth Union (consisting of the Rovers and Union clubs) and African clubs from Johannesburg and King Williams Town to represent them by proxy. Nevertheless, J. Joshua of the Progress club, seconded by Bud Mbelle, proposed that the new SACRFB be formed, and the motion was carried.

Robert Grendon from the Excelsior club in Beaconsfield was elected as the first president of the SACRFB. Educated at Zonnebloem College in Cape Town, Grendon was a teacher at the Beaconsfield Public School. He later taught at the famous Ohlange Institute in Natal, founded by John Dube, first president of the South African Native National Congress (later simply the African National Congress), and editor of its newspaper, *Abantu Batho*.[44]

Isaiah Bud Mbelle was voted in as the SACRFB secretary and D.J. Lenders and E. Heneke as auditors. The former was a foreman at a local 'Harness and Saddlery', while Heneke was a 'boiler' at De Beers, and secretary of the 'B' (or Coloured) Section of the South African League, a pro-British imperialist organisation formed to support Rhodes's adventures in Southern Africa. Lenders later became a prominent politician and the president of both the national rugby and cricket boards. In his capacity as vice-president to the legendary Dr Abdullah Abdurahman in the African Political Organisation (APO), Lenders was a member of the South African Native and Coloured Delegation which travelled to London in 1909. The journey was undertaken in a futile bid to persuade the British Parliament not to ratify the constitution for the new Union of South Africa until the discriminatory 'colour-bar' clauses in it were removed. The leaders of the new rugby board were, therefore, respected figures within the emerging black educated and political elite.

The newly-formed SACRFB decided to hold the first of 27 Rhodes Tournaments in Kimberley in August 1898. Bud Mbelle was instructed to inform the rugby fraternity of the plans and to send them the constitution once the committee appointed to finalise it had done so. He also had to see that the Rhodes Cup, which 'has been ordered from overseas', was acquired. When it arrived it was 'on two separate occasions exhibited to the public'. Bud Mbelle, in the meanwhile, was working hard travelling to and corresponding with other areas in order to ensure that they set up provincial associations and affiliated to the new national board. When the SACRFB met again in May 1898 there were representatives from Western Province, Eastern Province and Transvaal 'Coloured Unions' in addition to the GWCRFU, and all had paid their registration fees. These had also been the four constituent unions of the white South African Rugby Football Board (SARFB), formed a few years earlier in the same city. The development of sport in South Africa among both black and white was clearly influenced by broader patterns in the historical development of the country as a whole.

In keeping with the convention of the time, the SACRFB decided that 'an influential local gentleman' be asked to become a patron of the Board. The person chosen was William Pickering, brother of Cecil John Rhodes's closest friend and sole heir. Pickering later became secretary and a director of the De Beers Company.[45] Reflecting the paternalism of earlier Cape politics, it was common for prominent white politicians, local councillors and business people to be patrons of black sports associations right up to the apartheid era. The well-known historian Jeff Peires (referring to African rugby) has explained why this was so:

The game itself was played in appalling conditions. Most fields were without grass, and many were riven by ditches, located on slopes or acting as public thoroughfares. Boots were considered a luxury and each team had at most a single set of jerseys. Such circumstances bred dedication and selflessness: sacrificing one's wages to buy the team colours, walking all night to be at a match the following day. It also bred dependence on local whites. So much was so far beyond the reach of the average man – particularly when a large sum was suddenly needed for a special purpose such as a distant match or an anniversary celebration – that there was very little recourse but the 'benevolence' of the white man. One informant, who raised the money to take a Transvaal team on a tour of the Eastern Cape recalls, 'I had to cringe'. The chronic demand of black rugby for money and facilities meant inevitable dependence on whites. It also meant that prominent rugby administrators were either those who were [attached to institutions of learning or were] well off themselves, or excelled at least in asking whites for money.[46]

In many cases there were also social and political motives: the black elite was determined to win for itself a greater role in colonial politics and society, and this was one of the ways in which alliances were formed in an effort to advance its members' interests.

The donation of the Rhodes Cup, which the proud administrators stressed was more expensive than the Currie Cup, reflected the entry of a major new factor in black sport, namely big business and, in particular, the mining industry. Soon after the launch of the SACRFB and the presentation of the Rhodes trophy, Bud Mbelle and the Griqualand West Coloured Cricket Union approached Sir David

Harris of De Beers for a similar trophy for cricket. The union duly received a silver cup worth one hundred guineas, called the Barnato Memorial Trophy, in honour of another mining magnate, and initiated a national cricket body and tournament.[47]

Educational institutions were the breeding grounds for the new games and the ethos that went with them, although the initiatives in the formation of clubs, regional associations and competitions had come from the black elite themselves. However, from now onwards the mining industry played an increasing role in the development of black sport. It came to see sport as an important means of social control, not only helping to accommodate and channel the social aspirations and needs of the small petty bourgeoisie elite, but also to ensure discipline and productivity among the mass of non-literate menial workers. Under the compound system, hundreds of thousands of black male workers came to be housed in harsh, strictly controlled conditions. To deflect their attention away from the beer drinking, prostitution and faction fighting (and later also political discontent) that were common in the harsh mining environments, management initiated organised recreation. In the 20th century recreation facilities became a common feature on the mines and the mining houses organised and sponsored many competitions on a community-wide level. In this way the basis of sport amongst black people was widened with the result that black sports became more working class in nature. The mines began to influence the whole direction of sport in the black communities, including the sphere of rugby.[48]

The rise, fall and resurrection of the South African Coloured Rugby Football Board

The inaugural Rhodes Cup tournament organised by the South African Coloured Rugby Football Board in Kimberley from 20-27 August 1898 was a roaring success. Advertisements for the tournament were placed in the local Diamond Fields Advertiser and 'spectators rolled up in good numbers'. The mayor was in attendance to present medals to the winners and the South African rugby international, Chubb Vigne, was one of the referees. Western Province won all three of its matches to win the tournament.[49] The four team lists reflected the sporting demographics of the different regions as discussed previously: from the coloured/Muslim composition of the Western Province and Transvaal teams, to the African names of the Eastern Province squad and the fully mixed Griqua XV. The aim of the (SACRFB) was clearly to organise all those rugby players excluded from the whites-only SARFB. This was a significant achievement, predating formal political co-operation along inter-racial lines by nearly a decade; for it was only in 1907 that the South African Native Congress and the coloured APO held their first formal joint conference.

Soon after the first Rhodes tournament the South African war broke out, disrupting the normal activities of life, including rugby. The SACRFB suspended its national tournament for the duration of the conflict. The second tournament took place in 1903, the year after the peace agreement was signed. This was the beginning of a run of six tournaments in seven years held at rotating venues.[50]

After 1909 the SACRFB went into decline, virtually disappearing. Between 1909 and 1931 it organised only two tournaments, before coming to life again with five tournaments in that decade. Finance was one factor, as by 1913 the SACRFB was in the red by £11.1.6d. Internal tensions could also have contributed. But the outbreak of the first World War, which once again deeply affected South African life, must have been the main reason the SACRFB was crippled. Establishment white sport similarly went into limbo at this time as thousands of young men went off to fight in the war. No Currie Cup tournaments were held between 1914 and 1920 and no test matches were played between 1912 and 1921. The consequences for black rugby players were even more serious: the SACRFB only organised its first post-war tournament in 1928, 14 years after the previous one.

During the inter-war years black sport underwent interesting changes which were to have a big impact on the development of rugby in the black communities. The burgeoning Witwatersrand became a major focus for sport for the first time. Sport spread beyond the middle classes and soccer became a game of the masses overtaking cricket, rugby and tennis. Moreover, segregation, nationalism, internal dissension and growing numbers resulted in the emergence of new provincial and national sports bodies based specifically on racial lines.[51]

The South African Coloured Rugby Football Board, which had been particularly active during the early years of the century, was resuscitated again after 1928. In that year the Rhodes Cup tournament was organised again in Kimberley, which had to remain the permanent headquarters according to the terms of grant of the Rhodes Cup. Five more tournaments – held at irregular intervals in various parts of the country – followed in the next decade. The Rhodes Cup once more became an integral feature of the rugby calendar until the 27th and last Rhodes tournament held in 1969.

Scant information is available about how the SACRFB was reconstituted and who was involved. But it did not remain untouched by old problems and the broader political developments that were transforming sport. In 1936 the Board had to cope with two major crises. Firstly, African players broke away to form a separate South African Bantu Rugby Football Board. Secondly, a major realignment of forces in the Western Cape led to the formation of a new Western Province League. The founder members of this new super union were City and Suburban, whose vice-chairman Fred Russouw had initiated the move, Parow, Paarl and teams from other country districts. Later new unions joined until by 1960 the Western Province League 'controlled rugby in the Western Cape' apart from a few clubs falling under the jurisdiction of the predominantly Muslim Western Province Union.[52] Thus, the cultural- religious divides that had become clear in Cape Town by the turn of the century were accentuated, and two Western Province teams took part in the 1936 Rhodes Cup tournament.

After the 1938 Rhodes Cup tournament, the SACRFB elected a national team for the first time. The coloured springboks, as they were called, went on a hectic internal tour the following year. The captain was City and Suburban flyhalf Johnny Niels. Most of the players came from the two Western Province sides. The team travelled by train, playing nine matches along the line of rail in 21 days. The national side won the first six matches and lost two of the last three after injuries had necessitated the call up of eight replacements from Paarl.[53]

The idea was that the coloured springboks should also undertake a tour to England. Ever since the 1880s when John Tengo Jabavu, editor of the first independent black newspaper in South Africa, suggested sending a team of black cricketers to that country,[54] black sportspeople had expressed the desire for international contacts. The proposal for the coloured rugby tour was received with misgivings by representatives of the white board. However, when the Second World War broke out in September 1939, these plans became academic for the time being.

This was the third war involving South Africa during the course of the 20th century and once again sport experienced its disruptive impact. The national tournament was suspended for several years. After the war, the National Party of Dr Malan won the 1948 election and South Africa entered the violent and tempestuous era of apartheid. But, before dealing with apartheid's impact on rugby, events in the separate 'Bantu Board' require examination.

The South African Bantu Rugby Football Board

In the years after the turn of the century, African rugby in the present Eastern Province had continue to grow from strength to strength. By 1934 ten clubs were playing in the East London first league for the Martin Cup. Their were also leagues in places as far afield as Aliwal North on the Free State border and Umtata in the Transkei. The original inter-town tournaments were apparently still being held regularly and the game was now well established at educational institutions such as Healdtown and the South African Native College (later the University of Fort Hare).

Besides the rugby heartland in the Eastern Cape, the Transvaal became a new growth point for African rugby in the 1920s and 1930s. New clubs such as Swallows and United were formed by Eastern Cape people, and several mine-based teams emerged. In 1923 a Transvaal Rugby Union was formed. E. Juno Nogaga presented a cup for its competitions, which Swallows won in the first two years, beating four other teams in 1924. In 1925 the Native Recruiting Corporation donated the NRC Grand Challenge Cup. In the same year a combined Queenstown team toured Johannesburg and Pretoria to 'baptise rugby in the Transvaal which had just started ...'. By 1934 the Union had 15 clubs playing in A and B divisions. The growth of rugby on the mines was reflected by some of the club names: Wits Deep, Simmer and Jack, Geldenhuis Jumpers, etc. The annual meeting that year was held in the Bantu Men's Social Centre, the enclave for Johannesburg's black middle classes in Eloff Street in the very centre of the city. The minutes record that W. Gemmil 'Esq[uire]' and H. Wellbeloved Esq[uire] were the patron and honorary life president of the Union respectively. Mines, municipality and munificent liberals were strongly shaping the direction of the game amongst Africans.[55]

In 1935 the first Transvaal African provincial side was selected for a national tour. Reflecting the historical links, the first stop was the Eastern Cape. Starting in Aliwal North and going along the line of rail to East London on the coast, then inland again, Transvaal played nine matches on this leg of the tour, winning four, losing four and drawing one. The tour created considerable interest: the Lovedale authorities rolled out the red carpet, matches were played on white-controlled grounds, referees included ex-international Jack Slater, and in Adelaide the 'European public' turned out in force: 'all classes were represented and amongst those present was the Native Commissioner, the Mayor, members of the side bar, professional men as well as prominent farmers'. Transvaal completed its tour with a visit to Cape Town, where it heavily defeated Western Province three times, and a match against Griquas in Kimberley, which it lost.[56]

Following the formation of a separate South African Bantu Cricket Board in 1932, moves were by now under way to form a separate national body for African rugby as well. The brochures, reports and reminiscences collected by Braber Ngozi show that although African and coloured teams were regularly playing against each other at club level, and players from the respective communities were taken up in teams on both sides, the trend was towards organisational separation. Residential segregation was increasingly shaping the patterns of social intercourse and, in addition, the conditions were developing for the emergence of a more assertive nationalism stressing African self-determination. Sometimes the separation occurred amicably, for example when coloured players in Queenstown club left to form their own team. Sometimes strained relations caused the parting of the ways. In Cape Town in 1928 some (but not all) of the African rugby players who had been involved with the coloured Busy

Bees club formed their own club because 'they rejected coloured leadership'.[57] In the same year, five African cricket clubs broke away from the Metropolitan (Coloured) Cricket Union in 1928 to form the Western Province Bantu Cricket Union 'because they were not getting a fair deal both on the field of play and in administrative matters'.[58] According to one urban historian, the above developments were probably influenced by the 1923 Native Urban Areas Act, which led to the stricter enforcement of urban segregation; the Langa township was itself established in that year and soon people were forming area-based clubs.[59]

Early in 1935 Port Elizabeth administrators formed a committee to discuss the formation of a South African Bantu Rugby Board (SABRB). Further discussions took place at the inter-town tournament in East London. The board was formally launched in Port Elizabeth later in the year, during the inter-provincial cricket tournament. The local people were undoubtedly taking advantage of the fact that sports administrators from various parts of the country were going to be in the city. This showed at once how tightly knit the African educated elite of the time was, and how interlinked the organisation and interest in the middle class games of rugby and cricket were amongst Africans. The new president was J.M. Dippa of Port Elizabeth, who later became Native Welfare Officer for the Municipal Native Affairs Department in Bloemfontein. The secretary was Halley Plaatje from Kimberley. The son of Sol Plaatje, and the nephew of Isaiah Bud Mbelle, he was one of the driving forces behind the first national rugby and cricket bodies.

The first inter-provincial tournament to be organised by the new SABRB was held in Kimberley in 1936. At stake was the Native Recruiting Corporation Cup, donated by the Chamber of Mines. Eastern Province and Transvaal shared the honours after the final ended in a goalless draw. The other teams were the newly established Northern Eastern Districts union, with its headquarters in Aliwal North, and the home team Griqualand West; Kimberley declined as an industrial centre relative to the rapidly growing Witwatersrand in the 20th century, and was no longer the sporting force it had been at the turn of the century. For some reason Western Province, Border and Natal did not take part, even though the former had defeated the latter only the month before in a game in East London attended by 4 000 people.[60]

This was the first of 28 inter-provincial tournaments to be held in the next 38 years up to 1974, when a new competition, played on a home-and-away basis and sponsored by Bols Brandy (Stellenbosch Farmers Winery), was started. The inter-provincial tournaments involved a grinding schedule of matches over a period of one week. Sometimes teams played more than one match a day, particularly after a knockout competition for the Partons Cup was added to the league format for the NRC Cup.

The news reports of the 1940 SABRB tournament give a good indication of the ambience of these events and the level of organisation required. Considerable effort went into preparing for the tournament. The EP team was selected after trials involving teams from Grahamstown, Uitenhage and Port Elizabeth. Similarly, the Border team included 'many students from the Native colleges of the Ciskei'. The cost of organising the tournament was put at £200. Because of the war the board decided not to send round the customary subscription lists for financial assistance, but depended instead on gate takings. The usual enthusiasm for, and social importance of, sport was once again underlined: each of the six teams, consisting of squads of 25 players, played every day for a week and they were also entertained at a 'reception and dance' held in their honour in the East Bank Location. The power relations in the wider society were once again evident as well:

> When the Mayor opens the tournament at 2.30 pm today, with him will be the Native Commissioner, Mr D.G. Hartmann, the manager of Urban Native Affairs, Mr R.C. Cook, and the secretary of the [white] Border Rugby Union, Mr H.W. Wedd. There will be a separate entrance to the grounds for Europeans'.[61]

The white officials stated that the local council 'had always had the welfare of the natives at heart ... They would also be pleased to hear [that] ... the chairman of the Native Affairs Committee was quickly recovering after his serious illness (Applause)'.[62] It would only be in

47

the 1950s that black rugby players started challenging more aggress-
ively this sort of paternalism and discrimination.

The *Umteteli wa Bantu* newspaper described the condition of the
ground as 'atrocious'. Hartmann acknowledged this when he said at
the opening at Rubusana Park, 'I have heard the Bantu players are
tough men. To play on a field like the one here they will have to be
very tough'.[63] Nevertheless, there were 2 000 spectators in attendance
and the atmosphere was 'as tense as at an inter-varsity at Newlands'.
The crowd included a 'large number' of whites. Hosts Border ended
up winning the tournament. Star wing Braber Ngozi scored 33 points
during the week, a tournament record which was never bettered.

Studies confirmed that sport had became an important part of the
social life of the black townships by the middle of the 20th century.
According to a survey conducted by Prof B.A. Pauw in the late 1950s
and early 1960s, the majority of residents who had been born in the
East London townships (and could, therefore, be regarded as urbanised) expressed an interest in sport. Rugby was the most popular
game: about half of the people interviewed specifically mentioned the
game, and virtually all claimed to belong to a rugby club. The
under-35 age group and those who had an educational level of
standard five and higher were the most enthusiastic, but interest
extended along the whole spectrum of residents.[64]

Although only 12,5 per cent of the East London women interviewed in Pauw's survey expressed an interest in sport, some were
actually members of the local rugby clubs. In a strongly patriarchal
society, where rugby was a 'man's game' and 'women belonged in
the kitchen', women did not have the same freedom to play and follow
sport as men. When they were involved it was inevitably in support
roles: 'recruiting, cheering, laundry and also providing catering when
there were visitors', as the historian Rachidi Molapo has noted. Mr
M. Faku, an old stalwart of the Mother City club in Cape Town
recalled that the club started a women's section in 1968 and that 'we
never used to hire any ladies for washing our outfit after the match.
We used to collect all those smelling jerseys and took them to our
ladies' section and had them washed up'.[65] Ironically, the Western
Province Rugby Union was encouraging clubs to start women's

sections at the time because women 'were bound to the kitchen at the moment'.

As in any society, the rugby clubs reflected the broader dynamics of township life. In some, distinctions of occupation and social status played a role. For example, East London Stone Breakers was a club which attracted the 'more educated players'. In many townships sections of the educated and professional middle class strata held themselves aloof from other township residents. Placing great emphasis on speaking English, and priding themselves on being 'respectably dressed and gentle and polite in their manner', they were derogatorily referred to as the 'ooscuse-me' type.[66] The clubs in the local coloured communities also conducted their business in English, although the Cape Afrikaans patois was often the medium of communication amongst members.

The migrant labour experience, which underpinned segregation and apartheid, also had a big impact on rugby. Town dwellers and migrants from the country often belonged to different clubs. Mother City Rugby Club in Langa, for example, was 'exclusively' for people 'born and bred' in Cape Town. Thus, people were themselves perpetuating the distinctions made by the apartheid rulers between urban insiders and temporary migrants. A condition of membership was that 'the recruit should give evidence of having been in Cape Town for a continuous period of at least five years'. These conditions were very similar to those contained in the state's influx control measures.

Migrants in turn were usually organised on a 'home boy' basis, those coming from certain areas joining specific clubs. In Cape Town, the rugby and soccer clubs had tell-tale names like Transkeian Lions, Zulu Royals, Natal Wanderers, Basutoland Happy Lads and Bechuanaland Swallows. According to Wilson and Mafeje, as the numbers increased these would again split up into smaller units. For example, Eastern Cape people from the larger towns, those from rural villages in the reserves or bantustans, and those from small farming towns would split into different clubs. Harlequins broke away from Busy Bees because members from the larger towns like King Williams Town (*abantu basedolophini*) tended to dominate those from nearby smaller towns like Peddie, who they dismissed as 'pagans' (*amaqaba*). The Harlequins lived in Langa in the single-sex barracks and zones, while Busy Bees' members lived in better areas in Cape Town proper. Notwithstanding these differences, the members of the two clubs (because they came from neighbouring areas in the Eastern Cape) would still cheer on each others teams when they played against other Langa clubs.

According to Pauw, the 'home boy' tradition, which provided people with security in the often-difficult urban environments, also meant that a number of rugby clubs in East London were associated with 'particular tribal groups': Swallows with the Ndlambe, Bush Bucks with the Gcaleka from the Transkei, Tembu RFC with Thembu from Glen Grey and Cala, Black Lions with the Gqunukwebe from Middledrift, etc. However, these clubs were not confined to ethnic groups, and the majority were 'formed on some other principle'.[67] The United rugby club in Johannesburg was given that name in the 1920s because it members came from many different areas. And the Bantu Men's Social Centre was a place 'where any mention of tribal loyalties is deprecated and where English as a language is assiduously fostered in the belief that a common language will help to merge natives of different tribes ... into a Bantu nation'.[68]

Clearly, the rugby clubs were reflections of the myriad of influences shaping 20th century South African society.

Responses and realignments during the apartheid years

In 1948 the National Party won the whites-only general election, inaugurating the era of rigid institutionalised apartheid. Racial discrimination was extended and legalised in a way which was unique in world politics. The new government passed a barrage of segregatory legislation, including the Prohibition of Mixed Marriages Act, the Group Areas Act and the Bantu Education Act, until eventually there were more than three hundred laws controlling every aspect of people's lives from the cradle to the grave.

Apartheid soon gave rise to its antithesis: a powerful national movement in favour of non-racialism and democracy in South Africa. In 1949 the African National Congress adopted a new Programme of Action which rejected traditional moderate (and unsuccessful) methods of protest such as petitions and deputations to the authorities, and proposed the use of direct action through boycotts, strikes and civil disobedience in a 'mass struggle for national freedom'. The increasing influx of Africans into the urban areas in the 1940s meant that a basis now existed for the first time for a strong nationalist movement which could politically challenge white minority rule in an assertive way.

In 1952 the ANC organised a Defiance Campaign against unjust laws. Over 8 000 volunteers were arrested in a civil disobedience campaign organised on Gandhian lines. Volunteers deliberately offered themselves up for arrest, sitting on whites-only park benches, using whites-only railway facilities and otherwise flaunting apartheid laws. The volunteer-in-chief was a young lawyer called Nelson Mandela. The Defiance Campaign dramatically increased the popularity of the ANC. Soon afterwards the ANC joined with other pro-democracy Indian, coloured and white groups to form the Congress Alliance in order to ensure a broader campaign against apartheid. In 1955 the Congress Alliance adopted the historic Freedom Charter which spelled out an a new democratic vision for South Africa. The response of the apartheid government was to arrest and try 156 leaders in the massive Treason Trial which dragged on for years before all the accused were acquitted.

Sport in South Africa has always been linked to the social and political situation and, once again, both the application of apartheid and the intensification of the struggle against it had a direct bearing on developments in sport. From the late 1940s various racially compartmentalised black sports bodies sought to establish unity amongst themselves. They also began to seek international contacts, and to protest discrimination much more forcefully than before.

For example, between 1948 and 1958 the various black cricket and soccer bodies started playing inter-racial matches and forming new inter racial umbrella organisations – the new South African Cricket Board of Control (SACBOC) and the South African Soccer Federation (SASF), for example. These moves were in many ways similar to the multi-racial co-operation happening on a political level in the Congress Alliance during the 1950s.

In 1955 a young Port Elizabeth school teacher, Dennis Brutus, started the Co-ordinating Committee for International Relations in

Sport, the first organised sports protest group in South Africa. Its first success was in 1956 when the non-racial tennis association was given international recognition at the expense of the white organisation. Concerned by these developments, the government stepped in formally for the first time and announced an official government policy for sport. It reiterated that sportspeople should adhere strongly to the apartheid policies of the state. The government started harassing non-racial sports activists, *inter alia* by withdrawing their passports.[69]

Rugby did not remain unaffected by these broader political and sporting developments. In 1950 the South African Bantu Board initiated attempts to bring black rugby players closer together. In October that year the first 'test' between the national sides of the Bantu Board and the Coloured Board was played at the Showgrounds in Port Elizabeth. A crowd of 15 000 watched the Africans win by 14-3. Four more such 'tests' were held in the next two years. In 1951 representatives from the two national bodies formed a committee to organise a tour to New Zealand 'to play against the Maoris'. The estimated cost was £10 000. The following year the two boards decided to form a federation. Sipho Siwisa of the Bantu Board was elected as president with John Kester of the Coloured Board as vice-president. In 1953 a combined Federation team was selected. It was meant to undertake an internal tour, but this was cancelled 'because of racial tension in the country', a reference probably to heightened feelings following the Defiance Campaign.

The Federation, apparently formed at the initiative of the African body, was shortlived. Neither the New Zealand tour nor a Fijian tour to South Africa mooted for 1954 materialised, and no further 'tests' were held until 1957. The reluctance of Kester and the Coloured Board to co-operate was a major reason for the Federation's failure. The Coloured Board was still rebuffing African overtures at unity in the 1960s. An African rugby spokesperson complained that the coloureds were only interested in working together if they held the 'whiphand'. There were complaints that SACRB people were even unwilling to share changerooms and showers.[70] Despite growing anti-apartheid struggles, ethnic feelings and an awareness of 'the other' were still deeply ingrained. This also applied to the African rugby players. A rugby fan of that time recalls that though people were starting to talk unity, negative racial attitudes towards coloureds were fairly common.[71]

In a context where segregation and race were being practically enforced by law and projected as a historically given reality, non-racialism was a goal that had to be struggled for and self-consciously constructed . A further step towards non-racialism in sport was the formation of the South African Sports Association (SASA) in January 1959. SASA aimed to co-ordinate 'non-white' sport, to advance the cause of sport and the standards of sport among 'non-white' sportsmen, to ensure that they and their organisations received proper recognition here and abroad, and to pursue these aims on a non-racial basis.[72]

The national associations of eight different sports codes joined SASA, and amongst the patrons were prominent anti-apartheid political figures from the ANC, Natal Indian Congress and the Liberal Party.

The black rugby bodies were not among those present at the launch of SASA, but there were indications that the more militant politics of the 1950s was rubbing off on them. In 1959, the South African Bantu Rugby Board changed its name to the South African African Rugby Board (SAARB), showing its rejection of the racial epithets being used by the apartheid state. The president of the SAARB at the time was the East London attorney Louis Mtshizana. He clearly aligned himself with the intensifying struggles of the liberation movements. Under Mtshizana, the Board returned the Native Recruiting Corporation Trophy to the Chamber of Mines – it was replaced by the Zonk Trophy presented by a popular magazine – and in 1960 he called for rugby players to boycott the 50th anniversary celebrations of the Union of South Africa:

> *Celebrations run on the basis of apartheid may not be supported by an organisation that rejects apartheid in principle. What are we to celebrate? To the European folk it is the 50 years of prosperity that they have to celebrate ... To us [this] has been nothing else but 50 years of oppression and poverty ... We have no cause to celebrate ...*[73]

When SASA criticised the rugby people for having virtually been the only ones not to have initiated discussions with their white counterparts and for continuing to play inter-racial matches which perpetuated apartheid's racial categorisations, Mtshizana apologised to SASA secretary Dennis Brutus and said no such contests would be held in future. He made an impassioned plea for unity between the SAARB and the SACRB in 1961, saying that the only way forward was to 'emerge from our racial kraals and form a truly representative organisation, an organisation open to all racial groups on this basis of equality'. But the progressive voices within the rugby bodies were still in the minority. The racial contests continued and when Mtshizana was banned in June 1963 under draconian measures adopted by the apartheid government, the SAARB suspended him and elected B.D. Myataza as his successor.

The stab in the back for Mtshizana reflected the factional tendencies which bedeviled rugby administration for decades. Not only was unity between the SAARB and the SACRB not realised, but serious splits occurred within each of these bodies during the 1950s, 1960s and 1970s. Dobson details a number of cases in which disagreements within the African body led to personality clashes, disorderly meetings, suspensions, court cases, physical confrontation and breakaways. According to another informant, administrative matters often revolved around personality clashes, and the prevailing political attitude was that of resignation: 'we are playing along racial lines because that is the reality of the situation in South Africa'.[74]

The South African Coloured Rugby Board also experienced serious internal problems in the 1950s and 1960s. The most serious was the rift that appeared between leaders of the Western Province League and the Kimberley-based leadership of the national board. With 14 unions, nearly 200 clubs and 10 000 players, the League was by far the biggest affiliate of the SACRB. It was unhappy about the way the national body was run, and pointed to the SACRB's inability to progress financially and develop the game in other parts of the country. Although the Western Cape was strong, there were only a handful of clubs to be found in cities like Johannesburg, Pietermaritzburg and Kimberley. In 1954 the League drew up a memorandum calling for reform of the SACRB. When this was ignored by the

'Kimberley clique', which allegedly controlled proceedings via proxy votes at the meetings in that city, the officials of the League started canvassing support for a new national body.

In April 1958, the Western Province League, followed shortly afterwards by the Great Karoo Rugby Board and other small units, withdrew from the SACRB. In January 1959 the dissidents formed the new South African Rugby Football Federation (SARFF) at a conference in Paarl, the base of the new president, Cuthbert Loriston. Loriston remained at the helm of the Federation until his death in 1986. In later years he was pilloried for supporting the government's so-called multi-national sports policy and forming an alliance with Danie Craven's whites-only establishment SARB, but according to Dobson it was a power struggle between Loriston and Abdullah Abass (who later succeeded Kester as president of the SACRB) and not political or religious differences which were responsible for the formation of the new body.[75]

Thus by 1960 there were three national bodies catering for black rugby players. The new SARFF started its own Gold Cup inter-provincial competition to run alongside those of the SAARB (Zonk Trophy) and the SACRB (Rhodes Cup). In 1964 the first annual test match between the Federation and the African Board was played. The Africans also continued to play tests against the Coloured Board. However, the latter body and the Federation met only once, in 1964, largely because of ongoing tensions emanating from the split in 1958/9. Inter-race matches also continued at provincial level.

These inter-racial matches drew big crowds, and it is clear from the reports that the Africans, often assumed always to have been the cinderellas of South African rugby, more than held their own. For instance, in 1960 the Eastern Province Africans beat the Western Province Coloureds 9-6 before 12 000 spectators in Cape Town in a match which was meant to determine the champion provincial team in South Africa. The legendary flyhalf Eric Majola dominated the match. He and other stars of the 1940s, 1950s and 1960s are still remembered with reverence by many of todays' rugby pundits.

In 1963 the three black national bodies held discussions about unity, but nothing concrete resulted from this and subsequent attempts. Black rugby players also started making contacts with the white officials, but the SARFB continued to be guided by the rigid apartheid policies of the government.

If rugby players from the oppressed communities had been slow to respond to political events at first, growing polarisation within South Africa compelled them to take decisions from the mid-1960s to the early 1970s which clearly drew the lines between those supporting the struggle against apartheid and those throwing in their lot with the white SARB and government policies.

After the Sharpeville massacre of 21 March 1960, when police killed 69 people and injured 180 during an anti-pass demonstration, the state resorted to open repression to crush opposition to apartheid. It declared a State of Emergency and more than 18 000 people were detained. The ANC and the newly formed Pan-Africanist Congress (PAC) were banned. Anti-apartheid activists were forced to go underground or into exile. With legal avenues for change closed, the ANC and PAC embarked on an armed struggle. Draconian new legislation gave the state the power to detain people without trial, first for 90 and then 180 days. The knock on the door in the middle of the night and deaths in detention became more and more common. Sports activists were among those affected. Dennis Brutus, who helped start the South African Non-Racial Olympic Committee (SANROC) in 1963 to lobby for South Africa's exclusion from the Olympic Games, was shot by police and subsequently imprisoned on the notorious Robben Island. The secretary of SANROC, John Harris, was sent to the gallows for planting a bomb on Johannesburg station. SANROC was smashed and like other organisations forced to re-establish itself outside the country. It set up offices in London in 1966 where, together with the growing number of international anti-apartheid groups and the newly formed Supreme Council for Sport in Africa, it started co-ordinating a successful international campaign to boycott apartheid sport.[76]

The open repression of the 1960s was accompanied by a massive programme of social engineering as the National Party tried to reshape the country according to the grand designs of apartheid. Tens of thousands of people in the coloured and Indian communities were forcibly removed from their homes under the Group Areas Act after the suburbs in which they lived were declared white areas. Long settled communities in rugby strongholds like District Six and Parow in Cape Town were broken up. As people were scattered throughout the Cape Flats in areas with few facilities and infrastructure, established sports teams folded and rugby associations like City and Suburban and Parow and District lost playing fields they had used for decades.

Sports people in the rest of the country were similarly affected. The ferocity with which the apartheid government tried to enforce segregation and set up separate political institutions for the so-called coloured, Indian and African 'nations' created widespread resentment. Apartheid institutions were rejected from the start and increasingly the racial basis on which sports were organised in the black communities was challenged.

In 1966 the SA Coloured Rugby Board decided to change its name to the South African Rugby Union (SARU), dropping the racial designation it had carried since its foundation in 1896. In 1969 it replaced the Rhodes Cup, now recognised as a symbol of colonialism, with the SA Cup competition.

After the fierce repression of the early 1960s which temporarily smashed the radical challenge to apartheid, there was a resurgence of resistance in the late 1960s and early 1970s. This could be seen not only in the rise of the Black Consciousness movement led by the charismatic Steve Biko and the growth of black trade union activity at the time, but also in the re-emergence of a powerful non-racial sports movement within the country, reflected by the formation of the new South African Council on Sport (SACOS) in 1973. Within ten years SACOS, working closely with SANROC and international groups, exerted an iron grip over South African sport, as one establishment body after another was expelled from international competitions because of apartheid. SARU was a founding member of SACOS and although its relationship with this body was sometimes complicated, it soon became recognised as the one rugby organisation in South Africa which formed part of the 'people's camp'.[77]

SARU's gradual alignment with the democratic forces in South Africa not only gave it credibility, but also new impetus. In 1966, the City and Suburban Rugby Board left the Federation for SARU because of dissatisfaction with Cuthbert Loriston's autocratic leadership and the continuation of the racial matches between coloureds and Africans. In 1971 several clubs in Port Elizabeth broke away from the African Rugby Board's local affiliate and formed the Kwazakhele Rugby Union (KWARU) which joined SARU.[78] This brought a significant number of African players into SARU's ranks for the first time since the Bantu Board had split from the ranks of the predecessor Coloured Board in the 1930s. Within a year of joining SARU, KWARU reached the finals of the SA Cup. Further splits from the SAARB to SARU followed shortly afterwards in Uitenhage, Cape Town and other areas.

While SARU became firmly established as part of the broad democratic movement in south Africa, the Federation and the African Board responded to the political pressures of the time by moving closer to the white establishment. Playing as the African Leopards and the coloured Proteas respectively, the two boards became active participants in the new multi-national sports policy devised by the government and establishment sports bodies in the 1970s in an attempt to ward off growing international pressure. This policy aimed to relax the rigid segregation of the past by allowing limited contact at the national and international level without jeopardising 'traditional' policy at provincial and club level. The Leopards and Proteas were sent on tours abroad and given fixtures against international sides for the first time. A few players were included in non-representative South African invitation sides.

As old moulds were broken, new patterns became discernable in the 1970s. While SARU struggled to secure sponsorships and its players were regularly refused access to facilities by local authorities, the SAARB and SARFF received generous support from the state, business and the white SARB. The Mdantsane Stadium in East London, for example, was upgraded to the tune of R332 000 for the showpiece fixture between the Leopards and the British Lions in 1974. However, this unprecedented financial support could not neutralise the strong disapproval expressed within black communities about the participation of the two boards in multi-national sport. They were branded as sell-outs and as the lines were drawn droves of players left to join SARU. A rugby historian sympathetic to the Federation noted that by 1972 this body 'was on its knees':

*Clubs and unions were spilling over to SARU with its clear
anti-apartheid stance. The Federation stood accused of
being sell-outs and failures, giving the white administrator
an excuse to avoid full integration ... by giving the
Federation the sop of the odd overseas opponent.*[79]

The Federation and the African Board (now renamed the South
African Rugby Association, SARA) became almost totally dependent
on the white establishment. The main base for the former became the
coloureds-only Cape Corps military camp, 'beginning the army connection for the Federation'. The latter came to depend largely on
support from Bantu Administration Boards and the well funded, well
developed sports offices on the mines which became important con-
duits for channelling trained black sportsmen into multi-national sport
during the 1970s and 1980s.

In 1977 the SARFF, the SARA and the white SARFB united to
form the reconstituted South African Rugby Board (SARB). The lines
were clearly drawn. On the one side were the *status quo*-supporting
proponents of multi-nationalism and on the other the non-racial
SARU which closely aligned itself with the struggles of the resurgent
liberation movements. Relations between the two camps remained
antagonistic right through to the 1990s. Then the normalisation of the
political climate and mediation by the National Sports Congress and
the ANC's Steve Tshwete paved the way for rugby unity for the first
time in the long history of the game in South Africa.

As had been the case for over one hundred years, 'politics' had
the final say. One big difference now, however, was that the balance
of power had swung dramatically in favour of the oppressed since the
days when Isaiah Bud Mbelle and other pioneering administrators
head set out to establish the first non racial rugby bodies in the 1880s
and 1890s.

Notes

* The title of this chapter is derived from the Xhosa word for rugby, *mboxo*.
Encouragement and support from Albert Grundlingh and Zohra Ebrahim ensured
that I finally got down to writing this piece, and I also need to acknowledge the help
received from John Nauright.

A note is required on the vexed question of racial terminology in South Africa: black is used here to refer to all those rugby players who would have been classified as 'non-white' under apartheid. Non-racial (rather then black) rugby became the preferred term in later years, but it would be ahistorical to conflate the words non-racial and black when dealing with a century of rugby history. Although non-racialism was a goal from the start amongst progressive-minded rugby enthusiasts, there were periods in which black rugby players did not practise non-racialism, and even when non-racialism was assertively promoted from the 1950s onwards many black rugby players continued to support racial and 'multi-national' sport.

1. 'SA blacks not made to play rugby, says Uli Schmidt', *Cape Times*, 26 October 1994.
2. R. Archer and A. Boullion, *The South African game: Sport and racism* (London, 1982) pp. 8-9.
3. P. Dobson, *Rugby in South Africa: A history 1861- 1988* (Cape Town, 1989) p. 167.
4. Archer and Boullion, *The South African game* p. 8.
5. B. Ngozi, History and development of non-white rugby in South Africa (unpublished, n.d.). This is a bound source book, consisting of notes, newspaper reports, brochure articles and other miscellaneous pieces, which Mr Ngozi allowed me to copy in 1992.
6. J. Peires, ' "Facta non verba": Towards a history of black rugby', paper presented at the History Workshop, University of the Witwatersrand, 1981. A version of this paper also appeared in *Work in Progress*, April 1981.
7. See J. Morris, *The spectacle of empire: Style, effect and the pax Brittanica* (London, 1982) ch. 8.
8. A. F. Hattersley, *An illustrated social history of South Africa* (Cape Town, 1969) p. 221; and J. Hodgson, 'A history of Zonnebloem College 1858-1870, A study of church and society' (unpublished M.A. dissertation, University of Cape Town, 1975).
9. For a detailed history of early African cricket see A. Odendaal, 'South Africa's black Victorians: Sport and society in South Africa in the nineteenth century' in J.A. Mangan (ed), *Pleasure, profit and proselytism: British culture and sport at home and abroad, 1700-1914* (London, 1988). Many of the perspectives offered here were first developed in the above article.
10. Archer and Boullion, *The South African game*, pp. 22-4.
11. Dobson, *Rugby in South Africa*, pp. 167-8.
12. M. Galant, 'A history of Western Province cricket', (People's History Project, Department of History, University of the Western Cape, 1987) p. 2; and interview with Achmat Davids, Cape Town, 27 January 1995.
13. Galant, 'A history' p. 2.
14. Dobson, *Rugby in South Africa*, p. 172. For the 'Malay' connection, see also p. 171.
15. R.E. van der Ross, 'The political and social history of the Cape coloured people, 1880-1970 (unpublished manuscript, Institute for Historical Research, University of the Western Cape) part 3, p. 618.

16. Dobson, *Rugby in South Africa* p. 168, 171, 175.
17. Van der Ross, *'The political and social history'* part 3, p. 622.
18. Quoted in A. Odendaal (ed), *Cricket in isolation: The politics of race and sport in South Africa* (Cape Town, 1977) p. 23. See also *New Age*, 20 November 1958, p. 8.
19. APO, 'Football', 20 April 1912.
20. Dobson, *Rugby in South Africa* p. 170.
21. For in-depth studies of the early Western-educated elite and the process of political mobilisation see A. Odendaal, *Vukani Bantu! The beginnings of black protest politics in South Africa to 1912* (Cape Town, 1984) and A. Odendaal, 'African politics in the Eastern Cape, 1884-1912' (unpublished Ph.D thesis, Cambridge, 1983).
22. R.H.W. Shepherd, *Lovedale South Africa. The story of a century* (Lovedale, 1940) p. 508.
23. *The Kaffir Express*, 1 December 1970.
24. Cape archives, NA 467, Ecclesiastical 1875-1890, J. Buchanan to C. Brownlee, 21 July 1877.
25. See, for example, 'Ixesha le bhola, 1889', *Imvo Zabantsundu*, 17 October 1889.
26. See Odendaal, 'South Africa's black Victorians', pp. 199- 200.
27. Peires, ' "Facta non verba" ' p. 1; Dobson, *Rugby in South Africa* p. 201.
28. Ngozi, 'Black rugby Port Elizabeth', n.p.
29. Odendaal, 'African politics', p. 42.
30. Ngozi, 'Port Elizabeth black rugby', 'Black rugby in Port Elizabeth, 'Orientals Rugby Football Club' and 'History of Spring Rose Rugby Football Club', n.p.
31. 'Indaba', *Imvo Zabantsundu*, 29 May 1899.
32. 'Ibala lomdlala', *Izwi Labantu*, 12 June 1906; 'Iqakamba', *Izwi Labantu*, 30 April 1907; 'Eastern Province Native Rugby Union, *Izwi Labantu*, 28 May 1907.
33. Ngozi, 'Somerset East'. n.p.
34. *Izwi Labantu*, 23 March 1909.
35. *APO*, 19 October 1912; 2 November 1912; and 3 May 1913.
36. On the social life of the new black elite in Kimberley see B. Willan, 'An African in Kimberley: Sol T. Plaatje, 1894-1898' in S. Marks and R. Rathbone (eds), *Industrialisation and social change, African class formation, culture and consciousness, 1870- 1930* (London 1982), pp. 238-258.
37. 'Ibala labadlali', *Imvo Zabantsundu*, 1 August 1894.
38. 'Ibala labadlali', *Imvo Zabantsundu*, 26 August 1897.
39. Willan, 'An African in Kimberley' pp. 250-1, 257.
40. 'Ibala labadlali', *Imvo Zabantsundu*, 26 August 1897.
41. Willan, 'An African in Kimberley' p. 244; and T. Karis and G.M. Gerhart (eds), *From protest to challenge: A documentary history of African politics in South Africa* (Stanford, 1977), vol 4, p. 12.
42. 'A Rhodes Cup', *Imvo Zabantsundu*, 29 July 1897.

43. 'Ibala labadlali', *Imvo Zabantsundu*, 26 August 1897.
44. Willan, 'An African in Kimberley' p. 257.
45. Dobson, *Rugby in South Africa*, p. 169. For a profile of D.J. Lenders, see *APO*, 13 January 1912.
46. Peires, ' "Facta non verba" ' p. 2.
47. 'A Barnato trophy' and 'The Barnato memorial trophy', *Imvo Zabantsundu*, 2 December 1897.
48. Odendaal, 'South Africa's black Victorians' pp. 207-210.
49. Dobson, *Rugby in South Africa* pp. 168-170.
50. Dobson, *Rugby in South Africa* p. 170.
51. For more on the changing political economy and its effect on sport and culture during the inter-war years, see Archer and Boullion, *The South African game* pp. 118-124; and Marks and Rathbone (eds), *Industrialisation and Social Change*.
52. Dobson, *Rugby in South Africa* p. 171.
53. Dobson, *Rugby in South Africa* pp. 174-5.
54. 'Editorial notes', *Imvo Zabantsundu*, 9 March 1885.
55. Ngozi, reports from *Umteteli wa Bantu*, 18 April 1924 and 26 May 1934.
56. Ngozi, 'The Transvaal touring team, n.p.
57. M. Wilson and A. Mafeje, *Langa: A study of social groups in an African township* (Cape Town, 1973) pp. 114-5.
58. Odendaal, *Cricket in isolation* p. 308.
59. R.R. Molapo, 'Sports, festivals and popular politics: Aspects of social and popular culture in Langa township, 1945-70' (unpublished M.A. dissertation, University of Cape Town, 1994) p. 42.
60. Dobson, *Rugby in South Africa* pp. 202-3.
61. Ngozi, reports from *Umteteli wa Bantu*, 2 June 1940 and 8 June 1940; and 'Arrangements for East London tourney', n.p. The quote is from the first source.
62. Ngozi, 'Opening of tournament', n.p.
63. Ngozi, 'Bantu rugby tournament', n.p.
64. B.A. Pauw, *The second generation: A study of the family among the urbanized Bantu in East London* (Cape Town, 1987) pp. 44-5.
65. Molapo, 'Sports, festivals and popular politics' p. 49; and Ngozi, 'Oriental Rugby Football Club 75th anniversary brochure', n.p.
66. Wilson and Mafeje, *Langa* pp. 26-7; Molapo, 'Sports, festivals and popular politics' pp. 47-8; Nauright, verbal information supplied, Cape Town, 30 January 1995.
67. Pauw, *The second generation* pp. 172-3.
68. Archer and Boullion, *The South African game* pp. 120-1.
69. For a detailed discussion of the rise of the non-racial sports movement and the international anti-apartheid sports campaign see R. Lapchick, *The politics of race and international sport: The case of South Africa* (Westport, 1975).
70. Dobson, *Rugby in South Africa* pp. 204-211.

71. Interview with Professor Wandile Kuse, Stellenbosch, 21 January 1995.
72. Lapchick, quoted in A. Odendaal and P. Anderson, 'The non-racial sports movement in South Africa' (unpublished article, n.d.), pp. 3-4.
73. Quoted in Dobson, *Rugby in South Africa* p. 208.
74. Interview with Professor Wandile Kuse, Stellenbosch, +21 January 1995.
75. Dobson, *Rugby in South Africa* pp. 176-7.
76. For details of the boycott campaigns from the 1960s onwards see Lapchick, *The politics of race and international sport*; R. Thompson, *Race and sport* (London, 1964); P. Hain, *Don't play with apartheid: The background to the Stop The Seventy Tour Campaign* (London, 1971).
77. G. Standler, 'Of shop floor and rugby fields: The social basis of auto worker solidarity' (Institute for Advanced Social Research, University of Witwatersrand, seminar paper, 1994) pp. 14-19. @NOTE NO. = 78.
     For details of the KWARU break-away see Peires, ' "Facta non verba" '; Stadler, 'Of shop floor and rugby fields'; and Ngozi,'How KWARU came about', n.p.
79. Dobson, *Rugby in South Africa* p. 184.

CHAPTER THREE

The imperial heritage

Rugby and white English-speaking South Africa

Burridge Spies

The former Northern Transvaal and Springbok fly half, Naas Botha, recently maintained that rugby in South Africa is, to a great extent, the Afrikaners' game.[1] Many people in South Africa and in overseas countries would agree. When Chris Greyvenstein interviewed another famous Springbok fly half some years ago, he found that the English-speaking Bennie Osler discussed his cricket or racing experiences in English, but would abruptly swing into Afrikaans the moment rugby became the topic.[2]

English-speaking spectators at Loftus Versfeld join in the urgent chant of *'Nou! Nou! Nou!'* (the words do not mean 'No! No! No!', but are the Afrikaans for 'Now! Now! Now!') as Northern Transvaal or South Africa threaten the opponents' try line.[3]

The importance of rugby in Afrikaner society and the significant influence that Afrikaners have had on the development of rugby in South Africa cannot be denied. Yet the origins and early history of South African rugby, like the start of the sport in New Zealand and Australia, were part of the imperial heritage. Moreover, there is a rich English- speaking rugby culture and tradition – distinctive, but also part of the overall role of the game – in South African society.

It is not without significance that the first history of South African rugby, by Ivor Difford, and published in 1933, was written in English.[4] The original intention was also to publish an Afrikaans edition of the book and thousands of circulars and other forms were issued by the *Federasie van Afrikaanse Kultuurverenigings*. The response was so discouraging, however, that the Afrikaans version had to be abandoned.[5]

Beginnings

Tradition has it that the game of rugby originated at the public school, Rugby, in Warwickshire, England in 1823 as the result of the unorthodox actions of a schoolboy named William Webb Ellis.

This tradition was seemingly entrenched by a number of developments. In 1895 a plaque was erected at the school to commemorate Ellis' apparent feat. It stated:

> THIS STONE
> COMMEMORATES THE EXPLOIT OF
> **WILLIAM WEBB ELLIS**
> WHO WITH A FINE DISREGARD FOR THE
> RULES OF FOOTBALL AS PLAYED IN HIS TIME
> FIRST TOOK THE BALL IN HIS HANDS AND
> RAN WITH IT
> THUS ORIGINATING THE DISTINCTIVE FEATURE OF
> THE RUGBY GAME
> A.D. 1823

On 1 November 1923 a centenary match between a combined England-Wales team and a Scotland-Ireland team was played on the Rugby School field. This match, organised by the four British rugby unions, gave official sanction to Ellis' claim as stated on the school plaque.[6] Final recognition was apparently granted when the World Cup was designated the William Webb Ellis trophy. And yet the view postulated by two men steeped in rugby tradition – the journalist, John Reason, and the coach and rugby writer, Carwyn James – is that 'the more you study the history of football, the more unlikely becomes the assertion that William Webb Ellis was "the man who started it all" '.[7] A South African historian of rugby, Paul Dobson, suggests that the official acceptance of what he calls the 'William Webb Ellis myth' and the erection of the plaque at the school, two years after the formation of the Northern Union (the predecessor of the professional rugby league game) was 'a way of hitting back at the professionals.' It was a snobbish desire, he believes, to show that 'rugby football had mystic and upperclass origins unlike the league game, born of the money-grabbing of the working class.'[8]

Basil Kenyon's 1951-1952 touring team to Britain had a chant which they used at functions following the 'For he's a Jolly Good Fellow' sequence. 'What's he done for rugby? – blow-all', it ran. The mischievous rendering of it as they gathered round the William Webb Ellis plaque[9] may have contained more truth than they realised!

But if William Webb Ellis was not the originator of rugby, Rugby School did introduce a code of rules for a kicking and handling game.[10] There were in fact a number of different codes of football with constantly changing rules, played in Victorian Britain. It was one version of the game played at Winchester which was introduced to the Cape in 1861 by the new headmaster of Diocesan College (Bishops), the Reverend George Ogilvie (known as 'Gog', derived from his signature). This form of football played at the Cape became known as 'Gog's game'.[11] The first report of a football match on South African soil appeared in the *Cape Argus* of 23 August 1862 after a team of officers of the 11th Regiment had played a Civil Service XV at Greenpoint.[12] John X. Merriman, to become prime minister of the Cape Colony, and Louis Botha's rival to become first premier of the Union of South Africa – then a 21 year-old clerk in the Cape Colonial Office, distinguished himself, playing for the civilians.[13]

Some clubs and schools at the Cape favoured 'Gog's game', while others preferred the Rugby version. It was the influence of William Milton, who arrived in South Africa in 1878, which firmly swung the balance in favour of rugby (or Rugby). Milton, who had played fullback for England, became closely associated with the politician, capitalist and imperialist, Cecil John Rhodes. Milton, after whom a famous rugby playing school in Bulawayo was named, became administrator of Southern Rhodesia after the Jameson Raid and the 1896 Rebellion.[14] By the 1880s rugby was firmly established in the Western Cape, from whence it was spread by British regiments to the Eastern Cape. The first historian of South African rugby has stated: 'By 1890 the foundations of the Rugby game had been well and truly laid in one of the youngest of the British Overseas Dominions.'[15] These had been laid by British schoolmasters, soldiers, civil servants, miners and clergymen. Apart from Ogilvie, the future Bishops of Bloemfontein, Walter Carey, and of Pretoria, H.B. Bousfield, as well as the Reverend Adrian Roberts in Pretoria and the Reverend J. MacKenzie in the Free State capital, did much to help establish and encourage rugby.[16]

Rugby in English-language schools and universities

Bishops must be regarded as the pre-eminent South African rugby school. It played a leading role in establishing the game in South Africa. The green jerseys which have become the country's national colours were worn for the first time by a South African representative side in 1903. They were the colours of the Old Diocesan (OD) Rugby Football Club and were provided by a Bishops old boy, Fairy Heatlie, the captain of the South African team.[17] It is also claimed that Bishops has provided more rugby internationals than any other South African school.[18]

In fact, in many other areas of South Africa, schools, rather than clubs, may be regarded as the pioneers of the sport in their regions: Hilton College (whose black and white jerseys probably provided Natal with their colours), Michaelhouse and Maritzburg College in Natal, St Andrews (Grahamstown) and Grey High School in the Eastern Cape, and Queens and Selborne in the Border region.[19]

Every one of the 23 boys' high schools (both private and government) identified by Hawthorne and Bristow as possessing 'an ethos of excellence' have proud rugby traditions.[20] Similarly all the schools identified in 1974 as having educated the white English-speaking elite are strong rugby playing institutions.[21]

These elite English language private and state schools were influenced by the British public school model, including the importance placed on team games – particularly rugby and cricket ('the great game of empire'[22]). Rugby at Maritzburg College was considered to be 'a powerful binding force in the school'.[23] In rugby, it was stated 'the emphasis was placed on the team, not the individual' and that 'players will never wear numbers, at least not under the present headmaster'.[24] Rugby could, it was believed, provide 'a training in courage and self-control and the best sort of toughness'.[25]

Masters and boys at these schools believed in the exclusivity of their institutions. Peter Randall, author of *Little England on the Veld*, was taken to task for using the term 'Durban High'. 'DHS', he was instructed, 'is acceptable, but the best people in Durban speak only of "the School", for example, "What school is School playing today?" '.[26] At Pretoria Boys High the encouraging cry for their team is 'School, School, School'.[27]

Rugby at these schools was, and is, also associated with other features of the sport at British public schools like old boys' and house matches. Matches between old boys of the school and the school First XV have become traditional at many of the elite schools mentioned. They helped to extend the links between the schools and their former pupils, but it is surprising that hardly any old boys' clubs have become established in the premier leagues of various provinces. Inter-house matches were often fiercely contested. Paul Dobson writes that, in the 1959 season at Bishops, 'housematches played havoc with the start of the season as they wrote off several good players'.[28] Danie Craven, while teaching at St Andrews, Grahamstown, was so impressed with house matches at the school that he subsequently introduced the *koshuisliga* (residences' league) at Stellenbosch University.[29]

The *type* of rugby played at these schools was regarded as being as important as the game itself. Open, running rugby, played with *élan*, was the objective. 'All kicks are bad kicks', was the motto of a Bishops coach.[30] Pretoria Boys High, after winning the Transvaal Administrator's Cup for the fifth time in seven years, decided in 1933 to withdraw from the competition. Among the reasons given for the decision were the unhealthy spirit of cup-hunting and the dour type of rugby played in Administrator's Cup matches.[31] Similarly, not all English language schools initially made their players available for the Craven Week inter-provincial tournament for high schools.[32]

And yet success on the rugby field was considered to be important; 'a school's sporting prowess was taken to be "a more or less accurate indication of the tone of a school" '. When the Michaelhouse First XV had a poor season in 1950, the rector felt the need to report on the matter to the school governing body.[33] Schoolboys were aware of the need to give of their best on the field of play. Back in the 1890s Bishops prided itself on its players' tackling. The team's fullback related to Ivor Difford that after he had missed a tackle he was not allowed to speak in College, for a week, being told 'to shut up and learn to tackle'.[34]

The First XV Rugby Report of a famous school, which had not had a particularly successful season, stated:

> *The starting point is pride. Every player who represents ...*
> *[the school] at First XV level must have a burning desire to*
> *be the best ... Without pride there is nothing.'*[35]

Many rugby players from the schools mentioned retained their pride after they left school. Bobby Johns, a replacement hooker in Avril Malan's 1960-1961 touring team to Britain, stated that 'the greatest day in his rugby playing career was when he wore the Bishop First Team jersey for the first time ... more so when I wore ... the Springbok jersey.'[36] It has been suggested that one of the reasons why so few Old Edwardians have won Springbok rugby colours is that 'no subsequent experience can equal that of playing in the [KES First XV] distinctive red jersey!'[37]

The foremost memory of Kent Durr, former South African ambassador and high commissioner to the United Kingdom, of his schooldays at SACS was 'the smell of Wintergreen in the dressing rooms'.[38] But there were, and are other, voices which disapproved of the rugby culture at South African schools. As early as 1879, when the captain of football at Bishops asked Canon Ogilvie (dedicated to his 'Gog's game) if the boys could play rugby, he gave only grudging approval: 'Well, if you boys want to kill yourselves, do so!'[39] More than one hundred years later, Patrick Lee, writing of his first days at Hilton College in 1966, maintained that:

> *My immediate lessons were religious. The religion was*
> *called Sport. The holy altar was Rugby ... God was the*
> *Captain of the First XV. The angels were his team-mates ...*
> *Any boy who bunked watching a home game for the Firsts*
> *was flogged and cast into darkness, a hissing and a byword*
> *and probably a homo.*[40]

Even more recently, Tim Noakes, who holds the Liberty Life Chair of Exercise and Sports Science at the University of Cape Town, has expressed the belief that:

> *The over-emphasis on rugby at schoolboy level robs us all of*
> *a decent sporting education, thereby indirectly contributing*
> *to the general sedentariness of South African males.*[41]

However, large numbers of schoolboys were brought into contact with the game of rugby, not only as spectators, but also as players (even if only in the lower teams) at schools with proud rugby traditions. This has in many cases resulted in a lifelong interest in the sport.

Before leaving the subject of the influence of English language schools on the South African rugby culture (about which much more could be written), it is necessary to note that it was an old boy of one of these schools who probably made the greatest impact, not only on rugby, but also on other modern international sport. Peter Hain, now Labour MP for Neath in Wales, who played such a leading role in disrupting and preventing sporting tours to and from South Africa, received some of his education at Pretoria Boys High School.[42]

The two English language universities which have made the greatest impact on rugby in South Africa, are, first and foremost, the University of Cape Town (UCT) and then the University of the Witwatersrand (Wits). The 1920s with the Osler brothers, among others, at their disposal, have been seen as the golden age of UCT rugby.[43] Inter-varsities between Cape Town and Stellenbosch and between Wits and Tuks (University of Pretoria) became features of the rugby seasons in the Western Province and Transvaal. Wits had a mascot, Phineas, a seven foot wooden Highlander whose original is believed to have had connections with University College, London.[44] A special match between Wits and Tuks was arranged for the Prince of Wales (later Edward VIII and the Duke of Windsor) during his 1925 visit to South Africa.[45] Raids on rival institutions before matches, singing, cheer-leaders, revelry, drunkenness, and general misbehaviour were not unknown.[46]

Clubs

Clubs have been described as 'an alternative way of organising games which suit people who are not naturally thrown together the way soldiers and students are.'[47] Many of the South African rugby clubs formed in the third quarter of the 19th century were named after, or had connections with, British clubs.

The first South African club (and probably the first rugby club in the southern hemisphere) was the Hamilton Club, founded in March 1875, with its membership coming mainly from Green Point and Sea Point, Cape Town. The club was named after the Hamilton Club in Scotland, from which one of its founders, W. Nightingale, came. The establishment of Villagers by men who came from the southern suburbs and which had strong links with Bishops, was followed by the formation of Gardens and other clubs. In 1883 the first local football governing body in South Africa came into existence: the Western Province Rugby Football Union (WPRFU). In the same year, the WPRFU organised the first inter-club competition.[48]

British regiments introduced rugby to the eastern frontier, where the Alberts Club was founded in King William's Town in 1878. Other clubs were formed in Port Elizabeth, Queenstown, Durban, Pietermaritzburg and Bloemfontein.[49] After the discovery of diamonds, rugby started being played at Kimberley. The Pirates Club formed in 1884 owed its name to that most British of operettas, *The Pirates of Penzance* by W.S. Gilbert and Arthur Sullivan, which had been performed in Kimberley at the time.[50]

Another Kimberley club, De Beers, was forced to withdraw its team from the club competition in 1888 owing to a severe fire in a De Beers' mine shaft, in which some of their players were killed.[51] Rugby clubs were formed in Johannesburg after the discovery of gold on the Witwatersrand in 1886. Wanderers and another Pirates club (which developed links with Wits) were formed. Rugby players who worked on the May Consolidated Gold Mine started the Diggers Club.[52] In Pretoria the Harlequin Rugby Football Club was formed in 1902 after the South African War when many young men were drafted from the Cape Colony to the new Transvaal administration. Permission was obtained from the London Harlequins to use its name and colours.[53]

By the end of the 1880s rugby had become established in the major towns and in other areas of South Africa. Despite the acute political divisions which existed between the two British colonies – the Cape and Natal – and the Boer Republics – the Orange Free State and the South African Republic – it was decided to form a supreme governing body for all the rugby unions in South Africa. The result was the establishment of the South African Rugby Football Board in 1889. In the same year, Western Province, Transvaal, Griqualand West and Eastern Province played in the first tournament in Kimberley.[54] The stage was set for the first tour by an overseas team.

International tours

The first touring team consisting of England and Scottish players, and captained by W.E. Maclagan, arrived in Cape Town in 1891. Cecil Rhodes, no doubt aware of the benefits of such a tour in strengthening the imperial link, provided the financial guarantee to cover the expenses of the tour. The team played 19 matches, winning them all.[55] It visited the diamond mines in Kimberley and the gold mines on the Witwatersrand; its members met Barney Barnato and Paul Kruger. The social life, dinners, dances, picnics and smokers (concerts at which smoking – and drinking – were allowed), perhaps put more strain on the team than the travelling and the rugby. A member of the team recollected that the week spent in Johannesburg was the most hectic of all, but mused

that was not to be wondered at seeing that the wealth of the Witwatersrand had attracted some of the most adventuresome spirits from all quarters of the globe.[56]

Three internationals against South African representative sides were played at Port Elizabeth, Kimberley and Cape Town (all within the Cape Colony). Although teams from different parts of South Africa had played against each other since 1889, it was nevertheless remarkable that a 'national' side could be pitted against the tourists. 'South Africa' in 1891 was no more than 'a geographical expression' consisting of two British colonies and two Boer republics. It must have been gratifying to those politicians who favoured federation or union of the different communities on the sub-continent that players from such a conglomerate of states could represent South Africa.

There were no national selectors and the home unions were responsible for picking the South African teams. Not surprisingly no fewer than 28 players represented South Africa in the three matches, with local players tending to be favoured. Moreover, three different captains led South Africa in the three tests: H.H. Castens (who was also to captain South Africa at cricket) and who had aptly been educated at Rugby School, before going to Oxford; R.C. Snedden; and A.R. Richards (who was also to captain a Springbok cricket team). A further unique feature was that Castens, who had captained South Africa in the first international, was the referee in the third![57]

Sir Donald Currie, the Scottish shipping magnate and British M.P. who had wide business interests in South Africa, had presented the British captain with a gold cup with instructions to hand it to the region putting up the best game against his team.[58] Griqualand West was adjudged to have won that accolade. Conditions at Kimberley were undoubtedly important factors:

> *a ground absolutely destitute of grass, hard and covered with reddish dust ... a considerable glare ... [and] pillars of dust that rose up in the wake of the players as they ran made it difficult for the tourists, who could only manage to win by a converted try to nil.*[59]

Griqualand West handed the cup, another of the imperial links in South African rugby history, to the South African Rugby Football Board, to become a perpetual floating inter-provincial trophy.[60] Today, more than one hundred years later, the Currie Cup is still the premier trophy in South Africa's senior domestic competition.

Reason and James have pointed out that the relatively short boat passage between Southampton and Cape Town facilitated rugby playing contacts between Britain and South Africa.[61] After the 1891 tour, two further British teams toured South Africa. The 1896 team, captained by Johnny Hammond, was less successful than its predecessors, drawing one match and losing one of the four international matches to South Africa. In the wake of the Jameson Raid, Walter Carey, a member of the team who was to become Bishop of Bloemfontein, related that they

> *saw Paul Kruger sitting in state in the Volksraad at*
> *Pretoria: [the Reformers] Woolls Sampson and Karri Davis*
> *in gaol ... heard Sir Gordon Sprigg [the Cape premier]*
> *make a political speech ... and Sir Thomas Smartt opposing*
> *him.*[62]

The visit of the 1903 British team, captained by Mark Morrison, has been seen as 'a tour of reconciliation, rugby's contribution to healing the sad and painful wounds of the Anglo-Boer War'. Further South African goodwill may have been gained by the British team losing a number of matches – and the test series.[63]

Three years later the first South African team, captained by Paul Roos, toured Britain. This was the first South African team to wear the Springbok badge on its jersey, although the badge may have been worn by a South African racing cyclist, some years earlier. Paul Roos pointed out that the proper plural of 'Springbok' was 'Springbokken', but after their first practice, the *Daily Mail* called them 'Springboks'. As Paul Dobson has pointed out, Roos' name 'de-Dutched has stuck'.[64]

The Springboks won their first 15 matches and as the recorder of the tour reported, this led some journalists in Britain 'to write profoundly on national decadence.'[65] As John Reason and Carwyn James commented more than 70 years after the tour,

> *their forwards gave notice that sheer physique developed by*
> *a good diet and back-breaking manual work in the open ...*
> *would soon make them one of the dominant forces of the*
> *world.*[66]

It should be borne in mind that, in the wake of the South African War, there was considerable concern in British governing circles regarding the physical condition of Britons. Colonials, and South Africans in particular, in contrast, were regarded as being fine physical specimens: a report of an inspection in 1907 of the Michaelhouse cadet corps, related with awe that over 20 of the 90 cadets were over six foot tall.[67]

The tour was regarded as a resounding success which, it was believed, was not restricted to the victories (only two matches were lost) on the field of play. As South Africa was moving towards the formation of a national union, the effect of the tour on (white) racial unity was stressed. Paul Roos stated that 'the tour has united us. From Cape Agulhas to the Zambesi ... South Africa was one and all differences had been forgotten.'[68]

The Cape politician, 'Onze Jan' Hofmeyr, believed that:

They had made Dutch and English almost one ... whilst their poor petty statesmen and politicians – had been trying to do the same thing in the past in vain.[69]

One may leave the famous 1906-1907 tour with the comment, replete with unconscious irony, of a writer in the *Daily Telegraph* that they 'played in the best connotation of the familiar South African expression a real white man's game.'[70]

It is impossible to deal here with the varied impact of subsequent tours. It may briefly be noted that rugby contact with New Zealand was inaugurated with the visit of a services team to South Africa in 1919, a Springbok tour of All Black country in 1921 and a return series in South Africa in 1928. The first matches against an Australian team were played in 1933.[71]

In 1952, four years after Dr D.F. Malan's National Party had come to power in South Africa, that country's high commissioner in London, Dr A.L. Geyer, told a friend that his task, as a diplomat, had been made easier by the presence of Basil Kenyon's Springboks in the United Kingdom.[72] The same could certainly not be said of the Springboks' demonstration-ridden tours to Britain in 1969-1970, to Australia in 1971, and to New Zealand in 1981 when many inhabitants of the 'host' nations made it clear that a South African rugby team was most unwelcome in their countries.

The rugby men and politicians had also, of course, been too sanguine in 1907 when they stressed the unifying effect the Springbok tour had had on relations between the white groups in South Africa. Despite the subsequent formation of the Union of South Africa, English-Afrikaner disputes in the political and social spheres did not disappear.

Most Springbok teams have contained Afrikaans- and English-speaking players, with the former being in the majority in modern times. The Irish international, Andrew Mulligan, was, however, too sweeping and dogmatic, when he claimed, in a chapter entitled 'Of Rugby and Anthropology' that:

> It is relatively rare to discover English players in the South African scrum – except perhaps in the back row, where players like Stephen Frey [Fry], Basil Kenyon and Doug Hopwood can be found ... In the back line the names with a British ring to them are more frequent ...[73]

There have been some brilliant English-speaking Springbok backs, but there have also been some outstanding English-speaking forwards, even tight forwards, such as Harry Newton Walker, Okey Geffin, Don Walton, Mark and Keith Andrews, Guy Kebble, John Allan and Steve Atherton, to mention a few from more modern times. Reason and James claim that, during the 1960-1961 Springbok tour of Britain, there was 'a dichotomy [regarding the type of rugby that should be played] between the English backs and the Afrikaans forwards which was resolved in the forwards' favour'.[74] No confirmation of this statement could be found in other sources. It is also a fallacy to believe that English-speaking Springboks invariably opted for an open running game while the Afrikaners favoured a dour, kicking approach. The most pronounced South African exponent of the kicking game was the English-speaking Bennie Osler. A former New Zealand international claimed that the lack of enterprise shown by the All Blacks in 1937 could be attributed to the influence of Bennie Osler: the 1928 All Blacks, who visited South Africa are claimed to have returned home 'suffering from "Bennie Osleritis" '.[75]

Generally, it appears that there have not been rifts between English and Afrikaans players in Springbok teams.

In 1994, the Springbok captain, Francois Pienaar, said his team spoke a lot to each other in Afrikaans on the field; this, he maintained, was not 'sledging' the opposition or the referee, but encouraging each other and planning strategies.[76] Danie Craven related that the 1937 Springboks spoke English on the field to outwit their opponents: if they gave each other instructions in English, they would do just the opposite; if they spoke Afrikaans, they would carry out the instructions.[77]

There have been occasions when the South African rugby public has reacted to team selections along language lines. In 1955, when the Springboks captained by the English-speaking Stephen Fry and fielding largely English-speaking backs was struggling against the powerful Lions, the selectors received anonymous letters objecting that there were so many English players in the team.[78] Objections to team selections on provincial lines have been more common, though.

Playing in the old country

A number of English-speaking South Africans have represented England, and in fewer cases, Scotland, on the rugby field. The majority of those internationals were Rhodes Scholars studying at Oxford at the time they gained international selection. There are too many of these players to name them all in a short survey such as this and only a few special cases will be noted. Of particular interest is that of Stanley Osler, who had gained a Springbok cap in 1928 and who played for Oxford against the 1931-2 Springbok touring team, captained by his brother, Bennie.[79]

Many of these players who represented Oxford (and in some cases also, England) were invited to play for that remarkable club, the Barbarians. Formed in 1890, the Barbarians' motto, given to them by one of its earliest members, the Rev. W.J. Carey, later Bishop of Bloemfontein, stated that 'Rugby football is a game for gentlemen of all classes, but never for a bad sportsman in any class.' As Vivian Jenkins, the Welsh and Lions fullback, as well as a Barbarian, commented in the match programme for the 1977 Lions versus Barbarians match:

For the Barbarians ... it is a way of life that they play the game for the game's sake, with an emphasis on handling and running; and if defeat should come, well, the sun will always rise again tomorrow morning.[80]

Players from various clubs – in more modern times also from other countries – were and are invited to play for the Barbarians. Qualities of good fellowship, as well as rugby skills and panache were and are criteria for selection. Annual tours in Britain were arranged and in more recent times the Barbarians have also had fixtures against touring international teams.

One remarkable English-speaking South African, who played for Oxford, the Barbarians and England, was the Rhodes scholar and former Bishops' boy, Clive van Ryneveld, who also captained South Africa at cricket in the 1950s. Van Ryneveld, who became a United Party Member of Parliament and a founder member of the Progressive Party, would almost certainly have become a Springbok rugby player, had he not been injured.[81] But the English-speaking South African who played in the 'old country' and who best represented the Barbarian spirit, was another Bishops' boy, Harold Geoffrey (Tuppy) Owen Smith. In fact, Clive van Ryneveld was referred to by a British newspaper as 'a second Owen Smith'.[82] Owen Smith obtained blues for rugby, cricket and boxing at Oxford and captained England from the fullback position in 1937.[83] Before coming up to Oxford, he had scored a magnificent century in a cricket test for South Africa against England at Leeds, including being involved in a 103 run last wicket partnership.[84] Forty years after he captained England, he, above all other great players, was singled out in Queen Elizabeth II's Jubilee year as epitomising the Barbarian spirit. Vivian Jenkins, who played wicket keeper for Oxford when Owen Smith was in the team, related an incident in the match programme when they were opposing fullbacks in 1937. It was a fiercely contested rugby international between Wales and England at Twickenham which exemplified Owen Smith's character and typically 'Barbarian' attitude towards sport. During, half-time

Tuppy, still sucking his lemon, happened to look across in
our direction and catch my eye. At once came that
marvelous grin and wham! the lemon came hurtling in from

cover-point. I managed to take it, too, even without gloves
and whip off the bails, with I hope an answering grin of my
own. Then we were in the thick of it once again, at one
another's throats as it were ...[85]

The Barbarian tradition is yet another facet of British rugby culture which has spread to other parts of the rugby playing world, including South Africa. The South African Barbarians' tour of Britain in 1979 involved a team of eight black, eight coloured and eight white players, and was managed by the former Wits University and Transvaal loose forward, who was also an Oxford blue and a Scottish international, 'Chick' Henderson. The tour was deemed a great success. Black and coloured players gained experience of playing first class matches in overseas conditions, relations between team members of different racial groups improved, and the way was prepared for the Lions' tour of South Africa in 1980.[86]

Rugby and war

Links between sport and war have often been suggested. In the Australian context, a commentator in the early days of the First World War reflected on the purpose of sport as follows:

What is the good of games if they do not provide a training
ground for the sterner battles in our lives. If they do not give
us men whose hands they have taught to war and their
fingers to fight ...[87]

It is rugby, in particular, which has often been seen as possessing those attributes which prepare players for war. Stanley Osler, the Springbok centre and subsequently headmaster of Kearsney College, applied to rugby the words which the English poet and author, Siegfried Sassoon used in connection with fox-hunting: 'Images of war – without its guilt'.[88]

Writing about Natal, Rob Morrell has concluded that it is not possible to argue about the rugby playing schools in that region, as has been done about similar public schools in England, that they instilled in their boys a death wish which caused them to engage in risky sports and to place themselves in situations of danger.[89] Yet it was believed that rugby *did* prepare men for war. At the end of the First World War the following statement was made at a special meeting of the Natal Rugby Union:

> *Players almost to a man ... gave themselves whole-hearted [sic] to the Empire's cause. Rugby players throughout the world have proved themselves second to none in deeds of courage upon the battle fields of Flanders ... etc. and South African players have shown that they have been equal to the very best.*[90]

Certainly from the time of the First Anglo Boer War in 1880-1881, when rugby was played near the Majuba battlefield, until the Second World War, rugby players served in all the wars of the period. From the time that the Irish forward, Tommy Crean, a member of the 1896 British touring team to South Africa, won the VC at the battle of Elandslaagte on 21 October 1899[91], many rugby players have won decorations for bravery in various wars and sustained heavy casualties. South Africans (of course, not only English-speaking men) played rugby during war time in Flanders, France, Italy, Africa and in German prisoner-of-war camps.[92] There was particular rivalry between South African and New Zealand soldiers, who played matches against each other in Egypt, Italy and elsewhere during the Second World War. Soldiers from these two countries used to scrum down against each other when they met in pubs. There were ongoing arguments as to who possessed the mythical *Book*, supposedly the true source of rugby knowledge.[93]

On the domestic front, political factors during the Second World War led to splits in South African provincial rugby unions between pro- and anti-war factions. Matters were brought to a head by gate money at rugby matches being donated to the gifts and comforts fund for servicemen organised by 'Ouma' Smuts. Break away unions – the *Wes-Kaaplandse Rugbybond* in the Western Province and the *Oos-Kaaplandse Rugbybond* in the Eastern Province – were formed. The split was healed by the end of the war.[94]

Rugby in Natal and other outposts of the Empire

Before briefly discussing the rather special case of white English-speaking rugby culture in Natal, it is worth noting two further geographical anomalies regarding the organisation of rugby in Southern Africa. It has already been noted that, to all intents and purposes, rugby unification was achieved before political unification. A further anomaly is that parts of Southern Africa which never formed part of the South African body politic were part of the South African rugby body.

Basutoland (Lesotho) was regarded as part of the Orange Free State Rugby Union, whose official title was the Orange Free State and Basutoland Rugby Football Union; Swaziland was considered part of the Transvaal Rugby Football Union;[95] Rhodesian teams participated in the South African Currie Cup tournament from 1898 and the Rhodesian Rugby Football Union (established in 1895) was affiliated to the South African Rugby Football Board.[96] English-speaking Rhodesians, such as Ronnie Hill, Andy McDonald, Ian Robertson and David Smith, represented South Africa in international matches, while Afrikaans South Africans, like Salty du Rand and Ryk van Schoor, were living in and playing for Rhodesia when they first gained Springbok selection.[97] Rhodesian schoolboys played in the Craven Week tournaments. After Rhodesia became Zimbabwe in 1979, rugby links with South African were severed.[98]

The incorporation of Basutoland, Swaziland and Rhodesia as part of South African rugby can probably be ascribed to the initial widespread perception that the Union of South Africa was an 'incomplete dominion', and that in due course the Rhodesias and the high commission territories of Basutoland, Bechuanaland and Swaziland would become part of the Union.[99]

Long before the maverick Natal and Springbok loose forward of the 1960s and 1970s, Tommy Bedford, popularised the idea of Natal being 'different' to the rest of South Africa and that it was the 'last outpost of the British Empire', that belief was firmly rooted in Natal society. At a dinner in honour of the touring British team in 1910, the Natal lawyer and politician, F.S. Tatham, told the visitors that, when they got back to England, they should tell their kinsmen that there was no part of His Majesty's Dominions where the British traditions,

British sport and the grand old Union Jack were more revered than in the little province of Natal.

The manager of the British team responded that the captain of his team had remarked: 'These are the first real Britishers we have met in South Africa'.[100]

Rob Morrell's thesis that 'the spread of rugby in Natal has to be understood as part of a white, male, settler programme developed to meet the challenges of living in Natal'[101] is not acceptable. Rugby obviously spread and developed in many countries and in different situations and conditions throughout the world. M.C. Snell is more sensible when, writing about Maritzburg College, he stated that 'the average boy who played sport at College did so because it was compulsory or he enjoyed it ...'[102] But as Snell implies, rugby was an integral part of white male culture and there was, in rugby, as in politics, a particular Natal spirit of fervent support, of trying to play enterprising rugby coupled with a determination to be victorious. Pride was taken in the fact that it was the initiative of Natal officials and players which launched the South African Barbarians in 1960.[103]

According to the controversial Springbok wing, James Small, Natal rugby also inherited a feature of the British public school ethos: corporal punishment. In an interview with an Afrikaans magazine, he revealed that when a man is selected to play for Natal for the first time, he is 'initiated' by receiving three strokes with a cane.[104]

It should be noted, however, that the 'Britishness' of Natal rugby supporters does not extend to supporting British teams. During the 1974 Lions versus Natal match at King's Park, the crowd was so incensed when the Lions' fullback, J.P.R. Williams, punched Tommy Bedford, and other acts of violence, that they pelted the visitors with whole oranges to the extent that play was held up for some time.[105] The Natal Rugby Union commented on 'unnecessary fighting and fisticuffs by the visitors which was completely unnecessary and not in the interest of the game'.[106]

Natal rugby support and pride reached its height in 1990 when the team led by the English-speaking, Craig Jamieson, and coached by another English-speaking person, Ian McIntosh, unexpectedly beat Northern Transvaal in the final, to win the Currie Cup for the first time. On the Monday after the final, thousands of people lined the streets of Durban to give the team a ticker-tape victory parade and *The Natal Witness* subsequently published a lavish, illustrated book to commemorate Natal's triumph.[107]

The Jewish contribution

The Jewish population is a sub-group of English-speaking whites who need to be singled out for making a particular contribution to rugby in South African society. Numerous great Jewish Springbok rugby players, such as Maurice Zimmerman, Louis Babrow, Okey Geffin, Wilf Rosenberg, Syd Nomis, to mention but a few, have captured the imagination of the South African public. John Reason and Carwyn James found it curious that

> *The enormously talented Jewish people [who] have rarely been noted for very ardent participation in sport anywhere in the world ... have a great tradition of eminence in South African Rugby.*[108]

Some South Africans have at times expressed anti-semitic sentiments at the inclusion of Jewish players in the national side.[109] There is nevertheless quite a widespread belief among South African rugby followers that a Springbok team which does not contain a Jewish player is not at full strength.[110]

When Okey Geffin found that the first match of the Springbok tour of Britain in 1951 fell on the Day of Atonement, he declared himself unavailable for the game.[111] Louis Babrow's dilemma in New Zealand in 1937 was more acute. He was the best centre in the team; the 1924 and 1928 series between the Springboks and the All Blacks had been tied and the vital final test in 1937 was to be played on the Day of Atonement. As Danie Craven has related, Babrow decided to play, arguing that the time difference between the countries meant that when the match was being played, the Day of Atonement would not have dawned in South Africa, and as he was a South African, he was entitled to play in New Zealand.[112] Babrow played brilliantly and South Africa won 17-6.[113]

Rugby and soccer

In the early days, in some areas in South Africa, the two football codes managed to co-exist amicably enough. After the discovery of gold on the Witwatersrand, many young men played both 'the Association game' (soccer) and rugby on the same afternoon.[114] In the early days of rugby in Natal, that game was actually fostered by soccer clubs in Durban and Pietermaritzburg.[115] In 1906 the inter- town rugby match between Durban and Pietermaritzburg was preceded by a soccer match between Victoria and Mitchell Park Football Clubs. At the conclusion of their match, 'the Association players expeditiously removed the posts and nets and assisted the rugby men to erect their poles.'[116] At Grey High School in Port Elizabeth, both rugby and soccer were played initially, before the school switched to rugby alone.[117]

There was also, however, from the earliest times, intolerance and prejudice from both sides, but perhaps more pronounced from the supporters of rugby, regarding the playing of the rival code. Dale College, King Williams' Town, which became a proud rugby school, was originally a soccer school. Rugby was banned after 1886 and the headmaster, Bob Sutton, used to patrol the school grounds on a horse, 'looking for miscreants playing the forbidden game'.[118]

The antagonism between white rugby and soccer supporters was confined to English speakers and was, as Alan Paton has explained, grounded in class prejudice and snobbery. When he went to play rugby matches at Maritzburg College, he was watched by his mother and sisters, while his working-class father went to watch soccer. He has also explained that the young rugby players at Maritzburg College would become farmers, bank clerks, civil servants, magistrates and judges, lawyers, doctors and accountants, whereas the soccer-playing boys would become plumbers, electricians, bricklayers, barbers and bakers.[119] A further insight into the snobbery and class prejudice with which protagonists of rugby regarded soccer has been provided by another famous literary figure, the poet, Roy Campbell. Writing of his days as a pupil at Durban High School under headmaster, A.S. Langley, who had substituted rugby for soccer as the school's winter sport, Roy Campbell stated:

*He hated me with a deadly hatred from the beginning, not
for anything I had done, but that my father had founded the
Technical College, a soccerite school for poor children,
where they could be educated free.*[120]

The use of famous rugby grounds, Loftus Versfeld, Ellis Park and
Boet Erasmus Stadium, to play matches in the African Four Nations
soccer tournament in November and December 1994 seemed to signal
a new spirit of co-operation between rugby and soccer authorities.
However, class and race differences between supporters of the codes
soon surfaced. The South African Football Association executive
president, Solomon Morewa, took the corporate owners to task for
refusing to open their suites to their black employees to watch the
soccer.[121]

One development since South Africa's return to international
rugby is that the national team's two most recent coaches, Ian McIntosh and Kitch Christie, have been English speaking.[122]

If one conclusion, above all, emerges from this somewhat im-
pressionistic survey, it is the predominant role played by schools in
establishing and fostering rugby as a game among white South
Africans. With the changed conditions pertaining to, and about to be
implemented in, education, it remains to be seen whether those black
pupils who will be enrolled at traditional white rugby playing schools
will be converted to the game. Or will they convert the schools into
introducing soccer, as an addition to, or even instead of, rugby?

Notes

1. *Rapport*, 23 October 1994.
2. Chris Greyvenstein, *The Bennie Osler Story* (Cape Town, 1970), p. 31.
3. Personal observation.
4. Ivor D. Difford, *The history of South African rugby football (1875-1932)* (Cape Town, 1933).
5. Difford, *The history of South African rugby* p. ix.
6. Difford, *The history of South African rugby* pp. 8-11; Paul Dobson, *Rugby in Suid-Afrika. 'n Geskiedenis 1861- 1988* (Cape Town, 1989), pp. 9-10.
7. John Reason and Carwyn James, *The world of rugby. A history of rugby union football* (London, 1979), p. 27.
8. Paul Dobson, *Bishops rugby. A history* (Cape Town, 1990), p. 11.

9. R.K. Stent, *The fourth Springboks 1951-1952* (London, 1952), p. 41).
10. Reason and James, *The world of rugby* p. 27.
11. Dobson, *Bishops* pp. 15-16; Dobson, *Rugby* pp. 16-17.
12. Dobson, *Rugby*, pp. 17-18.
13. Phyllis Lewsen, *John X. Merriman. Paradoxical South African statesman* (Johannesburg, 1982), p. 19.
14. Dobson, *Rugby* pp. 20-21. C. Coggin, 'Milton', *Dictionary of South Africa Biography* (DSAB), Vol. 4 (Durban, 1981), p. 618.
15. Difford, *The history of South African rugby* p. 15.
16. Difford, *The history of South African rugby* pp. 151, 153; Dobson, *Rugby* p. 25.
17. Dobson, *Bishops* p. 44.
18. Peter Hawthorne and Barry Bristow, *Historic schools of South Africa. An ethos of excellence* (Cape Town, 1993), p. 40.
19. I.P.W. Pretorius, *'n Historiese analise van die betekenis van die geskilpunte rondom die Cravenweek vir hoërskole as interprovinsiale rugby-kompetisie*, unpublished DPhil thesis, University of the Orange Free State (1994), pp. 14-42.
20. The schools identified are: South African College Schools (SACS), Diocesan College (Bishops), Wynberg Boys High School, Rondebosch Boys High School, Paul Roos Gymnasium, Grey High School, St Andrews College (Grahamstown), Kingswood College, Dale College, Queens College Boys High School, Selborne College, Maritzburg College, Durban High School, Hilton College, Michaelhouse, Glenwood High School, St John's College, King Edward VII School, Jeppe High School for Boys, Pretoria Boys High School, Grey College, Kimberley Boys High School, St Patrick's Christian Brothers College (Kimberley).
21. H.W. van der Merwe *et al*, *White South African elites – a study of incumbents of top positions*, quoted in Peter Randall, *Little England on the veld. The private school system in South Africa* (Johannesburg, 1982), pp. 11-12. In ranking order the schools were Durban High School, SACS, King Edward VII School, St Andrews College (Grahamstown), Bishops, Jeppe Boys High, Rondebosch Boys High, Pretoria Boys High, St John's College, Michaelhouse, Kingswood College, Grey High School.
22. Dobson, *Bishops* p. 19.
23. Robert Morrell, *Forging a ruling race: Rugby and white, masculinity in colonial Natal, 1870-1910*, unpublished seminar paper, 1993, p. 13.
24. M.C. Snell, *The influence of the British public school system on Natal education: A case study of the evolution of Maritzburg College, 1910-1961*, unpublished BA Honours long essay, University of Natal, Pietermaritzburg (1992), p. 53.
25. Randall, *Little England* p. 121.
26. Randall, *Little England* p. 90, N7.
27. Personal knowledge.
28. Dobson, *Bishops*, p. 79.
29. Pretorius, *'n Historiese analise* p. 29.
30. Dobson, *Bishops*, p. 87.

31. Pretorius, *'n Historiese analise* pp. 57-58.
32. Pretorius, *'n Historiese analise* p. 115; Dobson, *Bishops*, p. 85.
33. Randall, *Little England* p. 121.
34. Difford, *The history of South African rugby* p. 553.
35. *The Pretorian*, 1989, p. 160.
36. Dobson, *Bishops* p. 231.
37. Hawthorne and Bristow, *Historic schools of South Africa* p. 195.
38. Hawthorne and Bristow, *Historic schools of South Africa* p. 18.
39. Dobson, *Bishops*, p. 25.
40. Patrick Lee, 'Scenes from a Natal childhood', *Style. Laughing through the turmoil. A collection of wicked wit 1980-1990*, p. 141.
41. Tim Noakes, 'Rugby rules, OK?', *Sunday Times Magazine*, 23 February 1992, p. 16.
42. Hawthorne and Bristow, *Historic schools of South Africa* p. 208; Gert Kotzé, *Sport en politiek* (Pretoria, 1978), pp. 125-133.
43. Howard Phillips, *The University of Cape Town 1918- 1948. The formative years, 1918-1948* (Cape Town, 1993), pp. 126- 127.
44. Bruce Murray, *Wits. The early years* (Johannesburg, 1982), pp. 375-376.
45. Difford, *The history of South African rugby* p. 615.
46. R. Archer and A. Bouillon, *The South African game. Sport and racialism* (London, 1982), p. 73; Phillips, *The University of Cape Town* p. 194.
47. Dobson, *Bishops*, p. 27.
48. Difford, *The history of South African rugby* pp. 12-13.
49. Difford, *The history of South African rugby* pp. 13-14 and *passim*.
50. F. van Rensburg, *G.W. Rugby. Die ontstaan en geskiedenis van Griekwaland-Wes-Rugby 1886-1986* (Kimberley, 1986), p. 287.
51. Difford, *The history of South African rugby* p. 78.
52. Difford, *The history of South African rugby* pp. 604-611.
53. Difford, *The history of South African rugby* p. 625.
54. Difford, *The history of South African rugby* p. 14.
55. Difford, *The history of South African rugby* pp. 15-16.
56. P.R. Clauss, 'Recollections of the 1891 British tour in South Africa', in Difford, *The history of South African rugby* pp. 256 and 251-259.
57. Dobson, *Rugby*, pp. 38-40.
58. Difford, *The history of South African rugby* p. 17; A.M. Davey, 'Currie', *DSAB*, Vol. 1 (Pretoria, 1968), pp. 192- 193.
59. Clauss, in Difford, *The history of South African rugby* pp. 252-253.
60. Difford, *The history of South African rugby* p.17.
61. Reason and James, *The world of rugby* p. 59.
62. W.J. Carey, 'The British tour of 1896 in South Africa', in Difford, *The history of South African rugby* pp. 269-270.
63. Dobson, *Bishops*, p. 44.
64. Dobson, *Bishops* p. 45; Dobson, *Rugby* pp. 59-60.
65. F.N. Piggott, *The Springboks. History of the tour, 1906-7* (Cape Town, 1907), p. 9.

66. Reason and James, *The world of rugby*, p. 58.
67. S.B. Spies, *The Union of South Africa and imperial defence, 1910-1914. Some considerations* (unpublished conference paper, 1981), p. 7.
68. Piggott, *The Springboks* p. 96
69. Piggott, *The Springboks* p. 105.
70. Piggott, *The Springboks* p. 120.
71. Chris Greyvenstein, *Toyota se Springbok-saga. Die verhaal in beeld van 1891 tot vandag* (Cape Town, 1977), pp. 64-71, 81-90, 104-108.
72. Stent, *The fourth Springboks* p. 59.
73. Quoted in Archer and Bouillon, *The South African game* pp. 63-64.
74. Reason and James, *The world of rugby* p. 141
75. Read Masters, 'Some impressions' in John E. Sacks, *South Africa's greatest Springboks* (Wellington, New Zealand, 1938).
76. *Rapport*, 20 November 1994.
77. Danie Craven, *Ons toetsprestasies* (Johannesburg, n.d.), pp. 35-36.
78. Danie Craven, *Die Leeus keil ons op* (Johannesburg, n.d.), p. 67.
79. Hawthorne and Bristow, *Historic schools of South Africa* p. 90; Greyvenstein, *Springbok-saga*, p. 270.
80. *Match programme: Lions versus Barbarians*, played at Twickenham, 10 September 1977, p. 5.
81. Dobson, *Bishops*, pp. 225-226.
82. *Evening Standard*, quoted in Dobson, *Bishops* p. 225.
83. Dobson, *Bishops* pp. 217-221.
84. Louis Duffus, *Cricketers of the veld* (London, n.d.) pp. 47-52.
85. *Match programme: Lions versus the Barbarians*, 10 September 1977, p. 6.
86. Carwyn James and Chris Rea, *Injured pride. The Lions in South Africa* (London, 1980), pp. 3-5; Dobson, *Rugby* p. 225.
87. Quoted in Michael McKernan, 'Sport, war and society: Australia 1914-18' in R. Cashman and M. McKernan, *Sport in history: The making of modern sporting history* (Brisbane, 1979) p. 3.
88. Maxwell Price, *The Springboks talk* (Cape Town, 1955) p. 52.
89. Morrell, *Forging a ruling race* p. 7.
90. Morrell, *Forging a ruling race* p. 18.
91. Difford, *The history of South African rugby* pp. 265-267.
92. Dobson, *Rugby* pp. 64-65, 85-98; Dobson, *Bishops* pp. 63-68.
93. Dobson, *Rugby* pp. 95-96.
94. Kotzé, *Sport en politiek* pp. 29-34; Dobson, *Rugby* pp. 86-90; A.C. Parker, *W.P. Rugby. Eeufees 1883-1983* (Cape Town, 1983) pp. 50-58.
95. Difford, *The history of South African rugby* p. 151; Dobson, *Rugby* p. 44.
96. Difford, *The history of South African rugby* pp. 183-193; Dobson, *Rugby* pp. 44-45.
97. Greyvenstein, *Springbok-saga* pp. 267-271.
98. Pretorius, *'n Historiese analise* pp. 82, 180.

99. Martin Chanock, *Unconsummated union. Britain, Rhodesia and South Africa 1900-1945* (Manchester, 1977) p. 10; L.M. Thompson, *The unification of South Africa 1902-1910* (Oxford, 1960) p. 269.
100. A. Herbert, *The Natal rugby story* (Durban and Pietermaritzburg, 1980) p. 165.
101. Morrell, *Forging a ruling race* p. 1.
102. Snell, *The influence of the British public school system* p. 56.
103. Herbert, *The Natal rugby story* p. 337.
104. *Rapport Tydskrif*, 10 July 1994 p. 7.
105. Personal observation.
106. Herbert, *The Natal rugby story* p. 393.
107. John Bishop, *Road to glory* (Pietermaritzburg, 1990).
108. Reason and James, *The world of rugby* p. 104.
109. Craven, *Die Leeus* pp. 92, 110.
110. Craven, *Die Leeus* p. 93.
111. Stent, *The fourth Springboks* p. 27.
112. Craven, *Toetsprestasies* p. 38.
113. Craven, *Toetsprestasies* pp. 32-43; Sacks, *South Africa's greatest Springboks* pp. 173-177.
114. Difford, *The history of South African rugby* p. 120.
115. Difford, *The history of South African rugby* p. 167.
116. Herbert, *The Natal rugby story* p. 131.
117. Difford, *The history of South African rugby* p. 602.
118. Hawthorne and Bristow, *Historic schools of South Africa* p. 100.
119. Alan Paton, *Towards the mountain. An autobiography* (Cape Town, 1980) pp. 30, 114.
120. Roy Campbell, *Light on a dark horse*, quoted in Hawthorne and Bristow, *Historic schools of South Africa* p. 141.
121. *The Pretoria News*, 30 November 1994.
122. See C. Steyn, 'Mac', *Personality*, 8 September 1994 pp. 28-33.

CHAPTER FOUR

Responses to isolation

Albert Grundlingh

Between 1970 and 1989, as international opposition against apartheid gained ground, at least nine official rugby tours involving South Africa were cancelled. The way in which the anti-apartheid movement abroad gained support and managed to exert pressure in ensuring South Africa's isolation, deserves a separate study; what concerns us here is how white South African society responded to its exclusion from the international rugby fraternity.

To rugby supporters it was a galling experience that their beloved Springboks were given such a torrid time by demonstrators during the 1969/1970 tour of the United Kingdom, the 1971 tour of Australia, and particularly the 1981 tour of New Zealand. This was the first time, since the introduction of television in 1976, that white South Africans could actually witness the chaos caused by that ill-fated tour. Bleary-eyed rugby supporters in South Africa, getting up early in the morning (due to the time difference) to watch their favourite game, were often greeted with scenes of clashes between police, pro-tour and anti-tour supporters, and pitch invasions by demonstrators. In the last test an anti-tour protester even made several low-flying sorties over the field at Eden Park, dropping flour bombs, smoke bombs and pamphlets on the field.[1]

Such displays provoked general condemnation from the white South African rugby public. Anti-apartheid protesters were seen as an ill-informed and manipulating minority. During the 1969/1970 tour of the United Kingdom, Gerhard Viviers, a popular Afrikaans rugby commentator, described demonstrators as the scum of British society who were sick in mind and body, 'pink British sewerage rats, whose protest should be summarily dismissed by all civilized people.'[2] Danie Craven regarded the boycott of South African rugby in 1973 as symptomatic of a 'sick world'. He continued:

> *What the pressure groups are after, not even they know.*
> *Behind all the demonstrations and shouting, primitive ways*
> *of expressing feelings, there must be motives which exclude*
> *sport altogether.*[3]

Such views reflect just how isolated South Africa had become from worldwide movements. Whereas in the rest of the world the 1960s were pre-eminently an era of social protest – expressed in student uprisings in France, Germany and America, and in the anti-Vietnam war demonstrations in America, as well as in cultural forms through anti-establishment music – in South Africa it was the high tide of ultra-conservatism and the entrenchment of rigid apartheid laws. Being hopelessly out of touch and isolated from universal trends, it is not surprising that at the time commentators in South Africa failed to come to an informed understanding of the wider significance of the campaign against South African sport.

Initially it was hoped that the 'outside world' would come to 'its senses', but after the cancellation of a proposed Springbok tour of New Zealand in 1973, it dawned on rugby supporters that the antagonism against racially selected sport teams from South Africa was much greater than they had anticipated. They also felt that rugby in particular was targeted for demonstrations. There was indeed some justification for this as anti-apartheid activists, in a somewhat oversimplified way, associated rugby exclusively with Afrikaners and apartheid. A journalist has explained that

> *apartheid carried an extra emotional charge when it came to*
> *the culture of The Game. It became the totem of white*
> *power, implicitly celebrated every time a whites-only team*
> *ran out in South Africa's name. It symbolised racial*
> *exclusiveness as a natural order of things – another dream*
> *of purity through sport.*[4]

It was the realisation that the anti-apartheid movement in sport was not going to disappear overnight that prompted the National Party government to modify its rigid sports policy. During the 1970s a complicated and convoluted re-formulation of National Party policy took place. Outwardly the impression of racially integrated sport had to be created. Yet this had to be done without actually sacrificing apartheid principles. As past masters in Orwellian 'new speak', National Party policy-makers devised the notion of 'multi-national' sport. 'Multi-national' sport was confined to a few special events at top levels only, leaving intact the apartheid pattern of sport lower down the scale; it entailed competition between the four main racial groups (white, African, coloured and Indian) representing separate 'nations', or between international teams from abroad and each of these groups individually. On the surface it could be seen as multi-racial sport, whites playing against coloureds for instance, but it was not multi-racial sport in the sense of people of many races freely participating together. Nor was it in any way non-racial sport, organised without reference to racial origins. Thus 'multi-national' sport, although it could be mistaken for multi-racial sport, was in fact a re-articulation of apartheid ideology. Indeed, as one observer commented at the time: 'To enter the realm of South African sport is to enter a crazy world where race shapes and distorts everything.'[5]

By and large in the early 1970s the organisation of rugby at the top level did not differ much from the government's 'multi-national' policy. Some coloured people played for the South African Rugby Federation (the team was called the Proteas) and African people for the South African Rugby Association (called the Leopards). On occasions these teams also went on separate overseas tours – the Proteas to England in 1971 and the Leopards to Italy in 1974. Critics regarded these tours as efforts by the South African Rugby Board to demonstrate that not only white, but also African and coloured people were sent on overseas tours; to those ignorant of the intricacies of South African society, these might have appeared as worthy attempts to promote African and coloured rugby, but in reality they perpetuated apartheid's racial divisions in sport. On tour, it was reported, South African authorities also tried to shield coloureds from too much contact with 'liberal' Englishmen. In addition to this, the Proteas, coming from apartheid South Africa and many being abroad for the first time, were socially ill-at-ease. An English coach, assigned to them, found that 'they were subdued, overawed in the clubhouse. They were like dogs, cowering in the corners of their kennels.'[6] The tour manager, Cuthbert Loriston, nevertheless claimed that the tour was worthwhile as it gave coloured players opportunities of broadening their outlook and gaining experience in a way which was not possible in South Africa in the early 1970s.[7] But that was precisely the essential political point that Loriston had missed – what the Proteas were experiencing in England was what they were legally and otherwise prohibited from doing in their own country. On their return, some of the Proteas were ostracised by their communities for going on the tour. As a result of such pressures, some Federation clubs also shifted their allegiance to the South African Rugby Union (SARU), with its unambiguous and uncompromising anti-apartheid stand. In the ensuing years the predicament of certain coloured rugby players, caught between opposing forces, remained much the same. Thus Errol Tobias, the first coloured Springbok rugby test player, found on the tour of New Zealand in 1981 that some members of the tour management discriminated against him, while at home his wife received threatening letters because he had gone on what was considered a racist tour.[8]

Already by the mid-1970s it had become clear that the 'multinational' sports policy of the government was not having the desired effect of countering the sports boycott. Craven's influential friends in the International Rugby Board, such as Albert Ferasse, president of the French Rugby Board, had impressed upon him the need to field a mixed team against the touring French in 1975. He took the advice to heart. Despite initial rebuffs from Prime Minister Vorster and the Minister of Sport, Piet Koornhof, Craven managed to obtain permission for a mixed team to oppose the French at Newlands.

In 1977 Craven also extracted government concessions for mixed national trials. On an organisational level the SARB, SARA and SARF amalgamated in 1978, though the white SARB tended to dominate in this arrangement. Craven, who had a good personal relationship with Abdullah Abass of SARU, also made overtures to this organisation in order to bring about unity. Abass (despite being rudely treated by Koornhof when he and Craven had earlier gone to see the minister in connection with mixed trials) carefully considered the possibility of such a merger. However, SARU delegates voted 12 against nine against further negotiations. Such discussions, they argued, should only take place once all apartheid laws had been repealed.[9]

Craven can certainly not be accused of a lack of trying in his efforts to bring about greater racial integration in South African rugby. In part he was hampered by a government which was slow to initiate change. But Craven himself was also overtaken by events. Particularly after the Soweto uprising of 1976, which in retrospect can be seen as the beginning of the end of apartheid, black demands for full political rights had gained momentum. Craven, though he publicly took an anti-apartheid stand, was in certain respects essentially conservative. He readily acknowledged the wrongs of apartheid, but as far as politics was concerned, as late as 1987 he was only prepared to support a qualified franchise for black people[10] – an option which the Progressive Federal Party, as the white opposition in parliament for the greater part of the 1980s, had already abandoned in 1978.

Craven's position on the vote indicates that he was out of touch with the dynamics of South African society during the 1980s as the country went through a period of dramatic and often traumatic upheavals. Support for a qualified franchise, amidst these circumstances, showed a limited understanding of the nature of black aspirations and the process of transformation that was underway. Indeed, in the most recent biography of Craven, P. Dobson, in an otherwise flattering portrayal, is not far off the mark in describing Craven's political outlook as naive.[11] At times Craven's suspect judgement of broader political issues meant that he was prone to antagonise sports activists. Thus, in the case of the Watson brothers of Port Elizabeth who were the first white rugby players to join the non-racial SARU in 1976, Craven – partly through a lack of understanding of the significance of this step – strongly opposed the move. As a result and although he might not have meant it to be construed in such a way, his position was taken as proof of racism.[12]

Craven was very active in the organisation of rugby clinics across the length and breadth of the country. Between 1982 and 1991 more than 314 clinics had been held and these were attended by over 88 000 players. These clinics involved children from all races and also led to senior feeder teams, mainly from the *platteland*, comprising white as well as African and coloured players. Dobson is convinced that 'Craven's enthusiasm for the clinics became a mission and was not related to tours from overseas.'[13] These clinics might indeed have assumed a life and ethos of their own, but it remains a moot point whether they would have started off at all had there been no international pressure on South African rugby authorities. The possibility exists that if Springbok rugby had not been threatened, there would not have been an incentive to embark on such a venture; in the 1950s and 1960s, before international pressures started to take its toll, little effort was made to promote the game to people other than whites. Perhaps Laidlaw's view, in a general comment on Craven's attempts to draw all races into the game, provides a more rounded assessment. 'Danie Craven', he wrote,

> *who, although his basic motive is the preservation of South African Rugby on the international scene, has been a strong advocate of multi-racial sport in the Republic and ... is a sensitive, humane and extremely idealistic man beneath his dictatorial facade.*[14]

A related question involves the impact of these efforts on race relations. One view is that sporting activities, as organised by Craven, helped to break down racial barriers.[15] The nature of the clinics, with youngsters from various races playing together without undue friction, might have created the impression of racial harmony. In a highly stratified society the importance of establishing areas of common interests cannot be summarily dismissed. Yet, under apartheid conditions and in the absence of meaningful social and political reform, sport could only have a limited impact. The structural constraints imposed by apartheid remained intact and were not threatened by sporting activities: African, coloured and white could play together, perhaps enjoy a beer together, but that was where it ended; they had to return home in their racially segregated trains, sleep in their racially defined suburbs and townships, and the following morning go to their places of work where their positions were also largely determined by race.[16] On the surface mixed rugby created the impression of equality, while in all other areas inequality was deeply entrenched. Rugby was powerless to change this, nor could it realistically be expected to do so.

Craven was prepared to go to great lengths to get South Africa back into international rugby. In August 1983 he was instrumental in arranging a huge press conference, lasting two weeks and involving 55 media people from different overseas countries in order to showcase the level of integration (for example, the clinics) that had been attained in South African rugby. The visitors criss-crossed the country in an expensive exercise totalling R750 000, but 'the rewards were well hidden, if they existed at all'.[17]

As black protest started to mount in the 1980s and South Africa moved into the spotlight of world media attention, it became increasingly difficult for the Springboks to compete internationally. Rugby administrators had to resort to all kinds of subterfuges; the Argentinians, for example, generally known as the Pumas, came out as the Jaguars in 1982 and 1984, supposedly representing South America.[18]

The greatest outcry was caused by the New Zealand 'rebel' tour of 1986. This took place in the wake of the cancellation of the official 1985 All Black tour which, to the great disappointment of the white South African rugby public, had at the last moment been stopped. For Craven, this was akin to a national disaster:

I knew people who actually cried openly – grown men ... It was a sad moment, and only when a country has actually experienced that kind of monumental disappointment can they appreciate just how South Africans generally and the SARB in particular felt that day.[19]

White South Africa felt it had deserved the tour. So did Louis Luyt, businessman and rugby administrator destined to become president of the SARFU. He was the driving force behind the 1986 tour which was arranged without informing the New Zealand or South African Rugby Boards or the International Rugby Board. The Yellow Pages directory was the main sponsor of the tour.

The tour temporarily eased the rugby hunger of white South Africans, but also reflected the tensions in South Africa at the time. The New Zealanders, travelling as the Cavaliers, were, with one or two exceptions, a full All Black side. They had a hectic schedule, crammed with tough matches, and adding to the pressure was constant police surveillance as fears existed that the tour might be violently disrupted. The captain, Andy Dalton, remarked that the demands of the tour had been so heavy that unlike other rugby tours, there has been little time for levity, to the extent that the coach, Colin Meads, advised the team to 'drink more beer' – an exhortation that Dalton drily noted, 'must have been a rugby first'.[20]

The tour took place at a time when black townships had become increasingly ungovernable as they refused to bow to apartheid laws and regulations. Shortly after the tour, the government imposed a suffocating national state of emergency which allowed for little political expression. Given these circumstances, it is not surprising that the tour, which took place in defiance of the international boycott, evoked strong reactions in black quarters. Ebrahim Patel of SARU condemned the 'deceit and secrecy' with which the tour was arranged and the 'callous disregard' it showed for the 'feelings and political realities of the oppressed people in South Africa.'[21] Sam Ramsamy of SANROC in London was equally scathing about the tour, but also made a wider political point that the tour had revealed the rugby establishment as desperate to obtain international tours. This was seen as a measure of the success achieved by the anti-apartheid sports movement abroad.[22] Although no large scale protest movements against the tour were organised in the country, some incidents did occur. In Cape Town opposition to the tour flared up, literally, as 700 pupils from township high schools took to the streets and set fire to a mound of directories of Yellow Pages, the chief sponsors.[23]

The tour had other repercussions. Although Craven was sidelined in the organisation of the tour, once the New Zealanders were in South Africa he gave the venture his full support. Craven was in London, attending an International Rugby Board meeting, when news of the tour broke. He was caught off guard, but ignored a request of the International Board that the players should be sent back to New Zealand. Craven argued that South Africa had deserved a tour by New Zealand and although he did not approve of the secretive way in which it had been organised, he regarded it as poetic justice after all the tours that had been cancelled as a result of anti-apartheid pressure. Craven's stance on this issue severely strained his relations with the IRB – a body which he had always held in high esteem.[24] In addition, there were strong and persistent rumours that the New Zealanders were paid to tour South Africa. Such allegations, however, were easier to make than prove. In another case, though – that of the 'rebel' tour by the South Pacific Barbarians in 1987 – there was more clear-cut evidence of money being an incentive to tour.[25]

These 'rebel' tours were expedient, short-term opportunistic affairs, and ultimately counter-productive, as they turned Craven's friends at the IRB against the SARB. In some ways rugby under the SARB was in a worse position after the tours than they were before the arrival of the Cavaliers. The deteriorating situation had a negative effect on preparations for the centenary celebrations of the Board in 1989 which were to include a World Invitation XV.

In their quest for international acceptance, the Board, and in particular Craven and Louis Luyt, now realised that they had to explore other hitherto closed avenues. It was under these circumstances that a series of meetings with the African National Congress in exile was arranged in, amongst other places, Harare. The ANC wielded considerable influence in the anti-apartheid sports movement, and Craven argued at the time that the route of South Africa's re-admission to international rugby was through Africa. This was a departure from the earlier policy of relying on 'friends' in the IRB.

Craven's contact with ANC 'terrorists' raised the ire of the National Party government (somewhat ironically because less than two years later the self-same government was to embark on full-scale negotiations with the ANC) as well as some of the Rugby Board members. The media, as was to be expected, made much of the meetings with the ANC, but in the end could point to little of substance that had emerged. Nevertheless, there is some indication that Craven's willingness to talk to the ANC had a beneficial effect on the opinion of overseas rugby people. At the time of organising the World XV for the Board's centenary, a prominent British rugby official was reported as saying: 'You should thank Dr Danie Craven and Dr Louis Luyt for the positive mood towards South Africa. The talks Dr Craven and Dr Luyt held with the ANC in Harare last year made all the difference.'[26]

The contact with the ANC can also be seen as a harbinger of developments that were to pave the way for rugby unity after 1990.

There is no clear-cut assessment of the efficacy of sporting sanctions, especially as far as rugby is concerned, in promoting change in South African society and politics. One commentator has argued that 'isolation prompted moves towards integration in the sports most affected by boycotts' and that 'by the 1980s the principle of racial integration in sport was widely accepted.'[27] As a general statement this is probably accurate, but it needs to be qualified. Attitudinal surveys have revealed that although the idea of integrated national rugby teams chosen on merit was favourably received, support for mixed teams on club and school level was much weaker.[28] At best, the country's exclusion from international sport had a differential impact on white attitudes. On a national level, mixed sport could be tolerated because it was an important showcase to the outside world, but racial mixing lower down the order was seen as another matter.

Equally problematical is the relative importance of sporting sanctions, and rugby in particular, in moving the National Party government away from apartheid and ultimately abandoning the system altogether. Authors John Nauright and David Black, though aware that the importance of the effect of the sports boycott can easily be overstated, nevertheless accord it a place. In 1993, they argued that:

> It is our contention that the generally unexpected decision of the De Klerk government to launch the current process of change cannot be understood without an appreciation of the corrosive societal and psychological effects of steadily expanding cultural sanctions. And of these, the loss of international rugby links, above all with New Zealand, were the most potent.[29]

Another author, Adrian Guelke, is less emphatic:

> Economic pressures, especially after the passage of the Comprehensive Anti-Apartheid Act by the United States in 1986, loomed much larger [than sporting sanctions] in both the thinking of whites and the calculations of the

> *government. Thus an explicit objective of the reforms*
> *embraced by ... De Klerk was to meet the conditions laid*
> *down in the American legislation for the lifting of sanctions.*[30]

Without any hard evidence on the deliberations in the inner circles of government during the last days of formal apartheid, a more precise evaluation of this issue is not possible. However, it has to be borne in mind that at the time the government was buffeted from all sides; as such, a variety of internal and external pressures combined to bring about change. In addition, and without wishing to deny the significance (albeit mainly symbolic) of the rugby boycott in a sports-mad country such as South Africa, economic boycotts during the 1980s had more serious and immediate repercussions. In the mid-1960s, when a New Zealand tour to South Africa was in jeopardy because of the possible inclusion of Maoris, Jan de Klerk, father of F.W. de Klerk, and Minister of the Interior at the time, told Craven that 'rugby was the least of his problems ...'[31] It would be surprising if his son, some 25 years later, had regarded rugby in a different light.

Rugby as popular Afrikaner culture

While rugby might not have been high on the agenda of apartheid statecraft, its enormous appeal as a form of popular culture during the years of isolation should not be discounted. Indeed, it can be argued that during the period 1970 to 1989 rugby as a cultural activity started to displace traditional and formalised Afrikaner culture such as *volksfeeste*. These festivals were usually associated with the 'sacred history' of Afrikanerdom's inexorable march to a supposed apartheid heaven on earth. The Day of the Covenant, celebrated annually on 16 December, glorifying the 19th century Great Trek as bringing 'light' and 'civilization' to the interior, was of particular significance.

From the 1930s until well into the 1960s the celebrations of the Day of the Covenant were important and well-attended occasions. In many ways these *volksfeeste* represented the high point of stylised public Afrikaner culture, characterised by an ideological blending of past achievements and current challenges. However, in the 1970s and 1980s, as Afrikanerdom became increasingly divided politically and as the country lurched from one crisis to the other, these celebrations started to lose whatever binding force they might have had. In the face of external sanctions, a declining economy and internal black insurrections, the past that had earlier made perfect ideological sense and that had projected Afrikaners as the 'natural' rulers of South Africa, now no longer seemed appropriate. Formalised Afrikaner popular culture started to loose its appeal.[32]

Moreover, interest in traditional festivities also declined as different leisure patterns, fueled by consumerism, emerged. Eugene Terreblanche, leader of the *Afrikanerweerstandsbeweging* (AWB), who in his fiery oratory made much of the 'sacred history' of Afrikanerdom, found that what he called the 'Coca Cola' culture muffled the sound of his ethnic drum in places like the Eastern Transvaal Highveld coal-producing areas. Commenting on this, a journalist noted:

> *Coca Cola, Lion Lager, colour televisions, micro-wave ovens, videos, fast cars and caravans – these are what concern the volk here much more than political ideologies or AWB rallies. Far from being traditionalists who reject the modern world, the Afrikaners here rush to acquire every latest bauble of modernity.*[33]

Whereas *volksfeeste* had become decidedly anachronistic for large sections of Afrikanerdom, rugby as a cultural phenomenon maintained its enduring attraction for Afrikaners. Rugby provided entertainment, it did not carry an overt political message – at a time when many Afrikaners welcomed a respite from unrelenting political pressure – and it provided an opportunity for predominantly male camaraderie and time-honoured ritualistic social behaviour. In short it was a *volksbyeenkoms*, a closing of the ranks, but without political soul-searching and sombre overtones.

Writing on sport as popular culture, an American author has observed that the 'sports carnival is, in a sense, a celebration, an escape into a fantasy and revelry, a brief relief from the mundane, often routine affairs and constraints of everyday living and working.'[34] Rugby as a cultural carnival in South Africa was no different. This was particularly noticeable during the 'rebel' New Zealand tour of 1986. Afrikanerdom might have been politically divided, the country gripped in a state of psychosis as black people forcibly challenged the structures of apartheid, and the tour itself highly controversial and 'illegitimate'. But all of this merely heightened the need of embattled whites for a momentary escape from the harsh realities of South Africa. A columnist in the Afrikaans press went to the heart of the matter when he reflected on the 'rebel' tour:

> *Whites certainly have a right to enjoy that which is 'lekker'*
> *[particularly pleasing]. Must we all sit in sackcloth and*
> *ashes and hypocritically mourn all the ills of this old world,*
> *all the lies and deceit, just because we live in South Africa?*
> *And do we have to keep ourselves from all the joys of life*
> *until the day that the supposed utopia ... of a non-racial*
> *South Africa will arrive, when whites will have to cede all*
> *the rights to a radical black clique? If the New Zealand tour*
> *can be a moral injection for this country – even if its only for*
> *whites – it would be a good thing. South African now needs*
> *every bit of positivism [sic] it can find.*[35]

Another journalist wrote with heartfelt emotion and more than just a touch of nostalgia on the eve of the test between the 'Cavaliers' and the Springboks at Newlands, Cape Town:

> *Along the touch line, thousands of people will get gooseflesh*
> *when the Springboks and All Blacks as elite inheritors of the*
> *long-standing rugby friendship, run onto the green turf of*
> *Newlands under the shadows of Table Mountain. There may*
> *be yellow stripes on the black jerseys of the All Blacks and*
> *the sponsors' logo next to our beloved bokkie on the chests*
> *of the Springboks, but that does not matter. Sports fans will*
> *be saying: 'Long live rugby between the Springboks and*
> *these All Blacks'!*[36]

It was the near obsession with rugby, to the exclusion of much else, that worried someone like Morné du Plessis, current manager of the South African squad for the World Cup. Du Plessis, a noted Springbok captain of the 1970s, who had run into trouble with the establishment for his anti-apartheid views, was of the opinion in the mid-1980s that white people, and particularly Afrikaners, made far too much of rugby. Rugby, he said, had become 'a symbol of our way of life', and the game was in danger of becoming associated with 'white dominance and arrogance'.[37]

The significance of rugby in a beleaguered society was underlined by the involvement of the South African Defence Force in the game. The Defence Force with a huge bi-annual intake of national conscripts did much to promote the game. Part of the reasoning was that rugby, as a disciplined team game, could help in the moulding of young men into soldiers. 'You can take a rugby player and within half an hour make a soldier of him', was the opinion of Magnus Malan, head of the Defence Force.[38] Apart from this, in the early 1980s, the Defence Force produced eight players for the Springbok team. Although this might have been a matter of pride for the Defence Force, for anti-apartheid political activists who viewed the Force solely as an army in the service of an illegitimate government, it provided ample proof of the close inter-relationship between the game and the ruling establishment.

Ultimately the only way rugby could rid itself of such perceptions was through the total abolition of apartheid. Even then, as we have noted earlier, the social history of the game cast a long shadow well into the post-apartheid era.

Notes

1. Several books and articles have appeared on the New Zealand tour. For a South African angle see W. Claassen, *More than just rugby* (Johannesburg, 1985) and R. Louw, *For the love of rugby* (Johannesburg, 1987).
2. G. Viviers, *Rugby agter doringdraad* (Pretoria, 1970) p. 101 *et passim* (translation).
3. South African Rugby Board Minutes, Microfilm 11, Craven's presidential report, 1973.
4. Quoted in W. Roger, *Old heroes: The 1956 Springbok tour and the lives beyond* (London, 1991) p. 34.
5. J. Brickhill, *Race against race: South Africa's 'multi-national' sports fraud* (London, 1976) p. 4.

6. Quoted in C. Laidlaw, *Mud in your eye: A worm's eye view of the changing world of rugby* (Cape Town, 1974) p. 189.
7. P. Dobson, *Rugby in South Africa: A history, 1861- 1988* (Cape Town, 1989) p. 184.
8. Laidlaw, *Mud in your eye* p. 189; Dobson, *Rugby* p. 184; Louw, *Rugby* pp. 147-148.
9. T. Partridge, *A life in rugby* (Cape Town, 1991) p. 100; P. Dobson, *Doc: the life of Danie Craven* (Cape Town, 1994) pp. 176-178.
10. *Sunday Times* 4 January 1987.
11. Dobson, *Doc* p. 135. See also p. 181.
12. *Vrye Weekblad* 28 July 1989; Dobson, *Doc*, p. 135.
13. Dobson, *Doc* p. 222.
14. Laidlaw, *Mud in your eye* p. 192.
15. Dobson, *Doc* p. 222.
16. Compare Partridge, *A life in rugby* p. 103.
17. Dobson, *Doc* p. 233.
18. Dobson, *Doc* p. 172.
19. Quoted in Partridge, *A life in rugby* p. 114.
20. *The Star* 27 May 1986. See also *New Nation* 6 May 1986.
21. *Cape Times* 1 May 1986.
22. *Post Natal* 26 April 1986.
23. *The Star* 17 May 1986.
24. Partridge, *A life in rugby* pp. 114-115; Dobson, *Doc* pp. 144-145; *The Star* 8 June 1986.
25. Dobson, *Doc* pp. 145-146, 148; Partridge, *A life in rugby* p. 114.
26. Quoted in Dobson, *Doc* p. 181. For the contact with the ANC see also Partridge, *A life in rugby* pp. 130-144; *Beeld* 5 September 1988; *Rapport* 11 September 1988; *Vrye Weekblad* 28 April 1989; *Die Suid-Afrikaan* December 1988/January 1989; A. Guelke, 'Sport and the end of apartheid' in L. Allison (ed), *The changing politics of sport* (Manchester, 1993), p. 168.
27. Guelke, 'Sport and the end of apartheid' p. 168.
28. Human Sciences Research Council, *Sport in the RSA* (Pretoria, 1982) p. 37. See also G.J.L. Scholtz and J.L. Olivier, 'Attitudes of urban South Africans towards non-racial sport and their expectations of future race relations – a comparative study' in *International Review for Sociology of Sport*, 19, 1984 pp. 131,139.
29. J. Nauright and D. Black, 'Much more than a game: Springbok-All Black rugby, sanctions and change in South Africa, 1959-1992' (unpublished paper, 1993) pp. 30-31.
30. Guelke, 'Sport and the end of apartheid' p. 168.
31. Quoted in Dobson, *Doc* p. 166.
32. Compare A. Grundlingh and H. Sapire, 'From feverish festival to repetitive ritual? The changing fortunes of Great Trek mythology in an industrialising

South Africa, 1938-1988' in *South African Historical Journal*, 21, 1989 pp. 19-37.

33. *Frontline* April 1988.
34. L. Kutcher, 'The American sport event as carnival: An emergent norm approach to crowd behaviour' in *Journal of Popular Culture*, 16, 1982 p. 39.
35. *Oosterlig* 25 April 1986 (translation).
36. *Die Burger* 10 May 1986 (translation).
37. *Die Suid-Afrikaan* October 1985 (translation).
38. Quoted in Roger, *Old Heroes* p. 203.

CHAPTER FIVE

Playing for power

Rugby, Afrikaner nationalism and masculinity in South Africa

Albert Grundlingh

Is there a link between rugby, Afrikaner nationalism and masculinity? The initial responses to this question could range from amused agreement to puzzlement or strong denial. In this chapter, I attempt to supply a more considered answer, starting with an analysis of the growth of rugby in Afrikaner circles. I then evaluate the dynamics of nationalism and the ethos of rugby culture, and look at how these two correlate with each other. Finally, I examine how the perceptions associated with rugby have helped to shape male identity.

Dissemination of rugby among Afrikaners

The role of the University of Stellenbosch in the Western Cape is the key to understanding the historical connection between rugby, Afrikaner nationalism and the dissemination of the sport among the *volk*. For the best part of the 19th century, Stellenbosch was considered the leading university in influential Afrikaner circles. It was to Afrikaners what the Oxbridge universities were to the national life of Britain and the Ivy League universities were to America.

Stellenbosch grew out of the Victoria College to become the first independent Afrikaans university in 1918. The University Council, representing the Afrikaans community, deliberately aimed to give the university a specific Afrikaner identity to counter that of the neighbouring and predominantly English-speaking University of Cape

Town. 'Stellenbosch', it was claimed later, was 'born out of the need of the Afrikaner volk.' As a 'true *volksuniversiteit*, it had to act as a steady light ... and beacon, illuminating the road of Afrikanerdom.[1] It was within this context that the game of rugby was played by the sons of the Afrikaner elite.

The first documented proof of a rugby club at Stellenbosch dates back to 1880, but the University Club was only officially founded in 1919. Rugby was already firmly established in Cape Town by the late 19th century, and its close proximity to Stellenbosch undoubtedly facilitated the development of rugby there. Stellenbosch had a head start over Afrikaner communities in the interior, particularly in the northern Boer Republics, where in some rural districts the game was completely unknown at the turn of the century.[2]

Stellenbosch was also the first and, for a while, the only institution where young, predominantly Afrikaner men were concentrated in one place for a reasonable period of time and where they had sufficient leisure to indulge in what has been called a game played 'by young males in a state of hormonal pugnacity'.[3] Rugby at Stellenbosch, however, was more than just an outlet for robust males in the prime of manhood. The game became part and parcel of Afrikaner student culture. One commentator regarded 'the way in which students could transform their fun and play into a reverberating cultural act, as one of the salient features of student life in Stellenbosch'.[4] With the rise of Afrikaner nationalism in the 1930s and 1940s, rugby became as much part of Afrikaner culture as *boeremusiek* (popular Afrikaner folk music with nationalistic overtones), *volkspele* (Afrikaner folk dancing), and celebrations like the 1938 centenary of the Great Trek.[5] The sport became part of a cluster of cultural symbols closely associated with a resurgent Afrikanerdom.

Two outstanding personalities who virtually became rugby legends in their own lifetime, A.F. Marköötter and, later, Danie Craven, did much to turn Stellenbosch into the Mecca of 20th century South African rugby. For Craven it was the 'task of Stellenbosch to train and provide players for the club, Western Province, and South Africa. But it also had to do more. It had to train players for other clubs and provinces.'[6] Stellenbosch Rugby Club regularly took the game further afield through annual tours to the Cape countryside, allowing people in 'areas deprived of the opportunities enjoyed by students' to savour what was considered 'sparkling student rugby'.[7]

The process of strengthening the rugby fraternity and enhancing the reputation of Stellenbosch spawned its own sub-culture, in which enthusiasm for rugby as an Afrikaner male activity was equated with robust patriotism to the exclusion of other, perhaps more threatening, world-views. F. van Zyl Slabbert, parliamentary leader of the white opposition in the mid-1980s, has graphically recalled how disillusioned he became with this sub-culture during his rugby-playing days at Stellenbosch in the 1960s:

> ... the post-mortems after the game with pot-bellied, beer-drinking 'experts' from way back; the sight of players continually ingratiating themselves with sporting correspondents for some coverage; the pseudo-patriotic ethos that pervaded discussions on the importance of rugby in our national life; seeing successful farmers grovelling at the feet of arrogant second year students simply because we were 'Maties' [nickname for Stellenbosch students] on tour in their vicinity. Mentally it was not only escapist, it was a social narcotic to anything else going on in our society ...[8]

The annual rugby tour was only one way of forging linkages between Stellenbosch and rugby on the *platteland* (countryside). More intensive and enduring was the role played by Afrikaans-speaking teachers and *predikante* (ministers of religion) in diffusing and popularising rugby on the *platteland*. Four years of teacher-training at Stellenbosch, and seven years of divinity studies for *predikante* at the Dutch Reformed Church seminary which was part of the university, not only equipped young men teachers and *predikante* with degrees, but added a thorough knowledge of and unbridled enthusiasm for rugby to their educational and theological armoury. From Stellenbosch they sallied forth to towns in the *platteland* where, as local notables with considerable influence, they encouraged and strengthened the rugby-playing fraternity. In the Karoo town of De Aar, for example, it was a source of pride that in the 1950s the four local *predikante* not only involved themselves in the game, but that between them they had a sufficient number of sons to field a complete team.[9] More generally, one author claimed in 1956: 'It is often said, with truth, that Stellenbosch-trained predikants and teachers have had the biggest share in making South Africa so rugby-conscious.[10]

The dissemination of rugby among Afrikaners in the Transvaal followed a somewhat different trajectory. Until the bilingual Transvaal University College was transformed into the more purified Afrikaner and openly nationalistic University of Pretoria in the 1930s, there was no single institution in the North which, like Stellenbosch in the South, could attract a large number of young Afrikaner men. Although competitive rugby had been played at the Transvaal University College since 1909, the institution was less of a focal point for the diffusion of the game in Afrikaner ranks and its influence less pervasive than that of Stellenbosch.[11]

While Stellenbosch was an almost exclusively student town, Pretoria was the administrative capital of the country after unification in 1910, and the subsequent growth of the city was closely linked to the expansion of the civil service and related government agencies. The majority of young men, including Afrikaners, who moved to Pretoria in the early part of the century, came in a working capacity and had less time for leisure activities than students. Those who were interested in sport joined open clubs like Pretoria Rugby Club or Harlequins, but rugby to them was less of an all-consuming interest than it was for students. The popularity of the game fluctuated between 1910 and 1919. However, it survived and began to flourish in the 1920s with the provision of better playing surfaces and through the energetic efforts of administrators, officials and certain players, many of whom had learned their rugby at Stellenbosch before moving to Pretoria.[12]

With the increasing urbanisation of Afrikaners during this period, concerted efforts were made to reach out to young Afrikaners who came from the rural areas and found themselves in a new and strange environment, and to introduce them to rugby as a game which could instill discipline and self-confidence. It was argued at the time that 'rugby is the best means of helping them to expend their energy that could otherwise steer them in a harmful direction.'[13] The process at work here was not that dissimilar from what took place in the United

Kingdom during the latter part of the 19th century when 'muscular Christian' priests, many of them educated at public schools, took an active part in diffusing rugby among the working classes. The game was regarded as a

> *means of moral and physical salvation, as activities which*
> *could help the denizens of the slums to become strong and*
> *physically healthy and to develop traits of character which*
> *would enable them to improve their miserable lot.*[14]

By contrast, in neighbouring Johannesburg, the city of gold and commerce, little was done to draw the Afrikaner working class into the game. The rugby clubs in Johannesburg were predominantly English speaking and middle class. More so than in Pretoria, members of these clubs saw little reason to concern themselves with the recreational activities of working class Afrikaners. Although individual Afrikaners excelled at rugby in some of these clubs, on the whole, until about the 1930s, rugby did not have great appeal for Afrikaners as a group in Johannesburg. Besides the fact that no real attempt was made by the clubs to popularise the game among Afrikaners in Johannesburg, working Afrikaners themselves had relatively little leisure time available to indulge in organised sport.[15] In addition, there was no Afrikaner educational or similar institution in Johannesburg at the time to promote the game.

This, however, should not detract from the fact that even at this early stage, after World War I, a number of Afrikaner players, mainly (though not exclusively) from the Western Province, rose to national prominence. After the war, sport generally experienced a revival and the visit of a New Zealand Imperial Services team in 1919 gave an added spark to the quickening of interest in rugby. This tour paved the way for the first South African rugby tour to Australia and New Zealand in 1921. Afrikaans speakers were well represented in Springbok ranks. Commenting on this, an Australian rugby critic was struck by the way in which

> *an essentially winter game can flourish in a hot country, and*
> *how it can attract men who have not a long heritage of*

British sport behind them ... For the Dutch [Afrikaans]
South Africans have taken to the rugby game as keenly as
their English compatriots. In fact, they seem to outshine the
English South Africans.[16]

During this period, though, rugby had not yet been invested with a narrow nationalistic Afrikaner ethos. The game was rather seen as an excellent way of promoting understanding between Afrikaans and English speakers and cementing a common bond between the 'two white sections' which could foster the notion of a white 'South Africanism', and could ultimately act in the interest of 'the higher scheme of imperial unity'.[17] Nevertheless, the fact that Afrikaners made their mark on the playing field in retrospect singled out the game as a sport with the potential to enhance the self-image of the Afrikaner.

Rugby and Afrikaner nationalism

Writing on the return of the rugby Springboks to the international fold in 1992 after 18 years of isolation, the British journalist, Frank Keating, reflected on the relationship between Afrikaner politics, nationalism and apartheid:

Rugby is the mother's milk, the lifeblood, the elixir that fuels
... [Afrikaner] arrogance. And clothed in their vestments of
green and gold, the Springboks are religious icons and
totems to the faith.[18]

This is an over-simplification of a more complex set of evolving beliefs, but it does capture some of the essentials of the intimate relationship between rugby and the development of Afrikaner culture and nationalism. It is not, however, a straightforward relationship. The reasons why a marriage between rugby and Afrikaner nationalism took place at all call for an understanding of the historical dynamics of Afrikaner nationalism and the ethos of the game itself.

The 1930s and 1940s were important years. Afrikaner nationalism at this time can be interpreted as a broad social and political response to the different facets of the impact of capitalism on South African society, which left certain groups, including a large number of Afri-kaners, stranded. It was within a context of increasing urbanisation and secondary industrialisation, as well as continuing British imperial influence in economic and cultural spheres, that Afrikaner national-ism made headway. Important ideological building blocks in this process were the promotion of a common language, the emphasis on what was perceived to be a common past, the unity of a common sense of religion, and the construction of what was considered a distinct and authentic Afrikaner culture.

A complex network of Afrikaner economic and cultural organ-isations was established and strengthened as a countervailing force to dominant British institutions and cultural practices. In the financial field, banks (such as Barclays Bank) and insurance companies (like Old Mutual) with large British assets were opposed by Volkskas and Sanlam respectively, which concentrated on mobilising Afrikaner capital in the interest of the *volk*. At another level, youth movements like the Boy Scouts had their Afrikaner counterpart in the *Voortrek-kers*.[19]

Representation of history played an important part in the construc-tion of Afrikaner nationalism. The 1938 centenary celebrations of the Great Trek, with nine ox wagons moving slowly from Cape Town to the Northern provinces, turned out to be unprecedented political and cultural theatre. The centenary trek, symbolically rooted in an ideal and heroic past, gave powerful expression to a desire for a more prosperous future, free of British domination. Pre-industrial 'pure' Afrikaner culture was emphasised and reflected in dress, dance and *Voortrekker kultuur* in general.[20] It also gave rise to a renewed interest in a sport like *jukskei* (a form of ten-pin bowling), which had claims of being an original *Voortrekker* form of recreation. After 1938, *jukskei* gained some foothold in Afrikaner circles and was organised and played on a competitive basis,[21] but in terms of the overall sporting scene it remained very much a minority interest.

It was rugby that continued to capture the imagination of many Afrikaners. The gradual Afrikaner appropriation of the game was not without paradox: given that the main thrust of Afrikaner nationalism was often directed against the perceived hegemony of English culture, why did Afrikaners show such a strong interest in a game that originated in England and epitomised the British upper middle class value system?

Even if nationalist cultural entrepreneurs had hoped to establish a completely new and authentic all-Afrikaner culture, such a project was not always feasible or viable. To create a pure, hermetically sealed culture is not easily accomplished; it is often more practicable to adapt, reshape and mould whatever promising material is at hand. In the case of rugby, Afrikaners had already proved that they could excel at the game, and it made sense to proceed from that vantage point.

The nature of the game itself also appealed to the evolving self-image of nationalist Afrikaners. Implicit in rugby is a certain duality. On the one hand, it can be seen as a collective sport of combat which emphasises stamina, strength, speed and courage; symbolically, the rugged aspects of the game could easily be equated with a resurgent and rampant Afrikaner nationalism. At the same time, despite being a rough affair, it was considered a gentleman's game and an excellent way of inculcating moral discipline in future leaders. These ambiguous qualities of rugby fitted in well with the physical, psychological and ideological needs of nationalist Afrikaners at a specific historical juncture. It is with considerable justification therefore that authors Archer and Bouillon can claim that rugby was a sport

ideally suited to ideological investment and the Afrikaners, who considered themselves to be a civilising elite, a pioneer people conquering barbarism, recognised an image of their own ideology in its symbols.[22]

In time though, as Afrikaners stamped their authority on the game, certain shifts in values and attitudes took place. Rugby might have originated in England and subsequently been exported to the colonies. But in line with the wider Afrikaner quest for independent nationhood, the game came to be an integral part of the attempt to transform and transcend the imperial heritage by reformulating and modifying the values associated with it. Whereas the British might have projected the game as a training ground for the inculcation and encouragement of values such as sportsmanship, gentlemanly conduct and fair-min-dedness, Afrikaners placed less emphasis on these and more on the game as an opportunity to demonstrate presumed Afrikaner qualities such as ruggedness, endurance, forcefulness and determination. Moreover, while the British regarded rugby as part of the imperial sporting ethos, confirming relations between the different sporting families of the Commonwealth, Afrikaners viewed the game in explicitly nationalistic and ethnic terms. Indeed, as one commentator has noted in general, 'the playing fields bequeathed by the Empire have become the symbolic sites of post-imperial struggles – for power, for identity, for the *style* of self-determination'.[23] This was particularly true in South Africa. In other Commonwealth countries, such as New Zealand, the desire for national self-expression through sport was still moderated by a relatively strong sense of imperial kinship.[24] But in South Africa, in Afrikaner ranks in the decades since the 1930s, Springbok rugby carried a thinly disguised anti-imperialistic message.

In analysing the linkages between the discourses of rugby and nationalist ideology it is possible, of course, to overstate the case. It can be argued that there is nothing particularly exceptional or significant in a group of people supporting their country's team in a specific sport. They do so for a variety of reasons which do not necessarily reflect a wider nationalistic ideology. J.G. Kellas has made the salutary point that

> the most popular form of nationalist behaviour in many
> countries is in sport, where masses of people become highly
> emotional in support of their national team. But the same
> people may display no obvious nationalism in politics, such
> as supporting a nationalist party or demanding home rule or
> national independence.[25]

In South Africa, however, the situation was somewhat different. Support for the Springboks was much more closely aligned to the overall Afrikaner nationalist enterprise in its various cultural and political manifestations. English-speaking South Africans might also have supported the Springboks, but their support was more muted, tempered by notions of friendly rivalry between different common-wealth countries. For many Afrikaners, this was not the case; support for the Springboks was on the same continuum as membership of the National Party.

For Afrikaners who felt themselves oppressed and disadvantaged by the continuing British influence in South Africa, rugby created an opportunity to beat the English at their own game. It is no surprise that rivalry between Afrikaans and English speakers was particularly fierce on the playing fields. Clashes between Afrikaans and English schools, universities and clubs gave the lie to the cliché that rugby was 'only a game'. One 'participant-observer' at an inter-varsity game between the University of the Witwatersrand and the University of Pretoria, after the latter had become an autonomous Afrikaner university in the 1930s, has recalled:

> When Witwatersrand played Pretoria, it wasn't just rugby they were playing, there was an enmity and a bitterness and a hatred of each other. The overtones were quite clear. The major goal was to beat the other university not only in the game. I think the competition between two such universities was naturally bitter ... because it was the child of the hatred of the Afrikaans – or the English-speaking. It certainly didn't dissipate the tension.[26]

Much the same could be said for the annual inter- varsities between the Universities of Cape Town and Stellenbosch.[27] When South Africa competed internationally, the outcome of matches against British teams was of more than just sporting interest. The Springbok tour to Britain in 1951-52, which saw the South Africans winning 30 out of 31 games, was hailed as a major national triumph; by contrast, when the Springboks lost two test matches against the British Lions during the 1955 tour of South Africa, the result was met with stunned disbelief: 'How has it happened that a *boer* has been defeated by an Englishman on the rugby field?'[28] Some players even received death threats from the public for bringing the 'national game' into disrepute by losing against the British.[29]

While Afrikaner-English rivalry was real enough, Afrikaners shared the middle class character of the game with their English counterparts. The steady upward mobility of Afrikaners, particularly under a sympathetic government in power from 1948 onwards, was accompanied by the proliferation of Afrikaner educational institutions with rugby as the main winter game. The pool of potential rugby players from a burgeoning middle class constantly grew. Commenting on the 1956 Springbok tour to Australia and New Zealand, G. Hogg, chairman of the New Zealand Rugby Council, considered the Springboks to be 'mostly the educated type, whilst the All Blacks are mostly workmen who were used to a hard life'.[30] It was difficult for a player not comfortably employed or who did not have some means of private income or other form of assistance to play top-level rugby for an extended period. This prompted Martin Pelser, a prominent Springbok flank forward in the 1960s who had turned to professional rugby, to remark on the class nature of the union game:

I cannot recount the many days of unpaid leave I had to take
for the sake of amateur rugby ... Amateur rugby, and
especially Springbok rugby, is a game for rich men's sons.
I, and others like me, could no longer afford it.[31]

In the early 1970s, half of the provincial rugby players could be classified as white collar workers, 21 per cent as professionals, ten per cent as students, eight per cent as farmers, and under ten per cent as blue collar workers.[32] While these statistics are revealing, it has to be borne in mind that in certain areas like Despatch and Uitenhage in the Eastern Cape, the game had a considerable following amongst the white working class employed in the motor manufacturing industry.

In general, soccer did not enjoy the same middle class status as rugby among Afrikaners. Working class children of the 1920s and early 1930s, living in cities like Cape Town, often played soccer instead of rugby. This was mainly because, in the absence of grass playing fields or large suburban lawns, it was easier to kick a soccer ball in some dusty and stony backstreet than to play a hard, physical game like rugby on an unyielding surface.[33] With the rise of organised Afrikanerdom and an assertive middle class, soccer's working class origins were frowned upon. Moreover, the fact that soccer was a very popular sport among black people gave it, in an increasingly racially stratified society, the tag of being a 'black man's game'.[34]

The middle class character of rugby facilitated its acceptance as a constituent part of the white, and especially Afrikaner, establishment. Many of the players came from more or less the same background, and shared the same values. To play rugby was a respectable pastime that met with the approval and confirmation of wider society. 'Mr Rugby' himself, Danie Craven, recalled that in his playing days in the 1930s, the word 'rugby' was a name 'to conjure' with, a magical word, and a rugby player was admired by all and sundry.[35] Admittedly, not all the spectators were middle class, but they were sufficiently ethnically integrated into Afrikaner society not to allow matters of class to affect their support of the game.

The way Afrikaner rugby meshed with the establishment fitted in with the general sociological pattern discernible in other rugby-playing countries. In 1974 Chris Laidlaw, a New Zealand scrumhalf and Oxford scholar, noted in no uncertain terms that:

> A central reason for rugby's international conformity, is the
> fact that it is, universally, an establishment activity.
> Distressingly so. It is normally played and administered by
> conservative elements in society. The ... 'rugger buggers' of
> today are far from radical; rugby's tradition would hardly
> have survived if they were. They are acquiring reputations
> as thundering bores with short hair and a suspicion of
> 'lefties'. Today's players are by and large tomorrow's
> Tories.[36]

Likewise, in the South African context, it has been claimed that players generally hold conservative world views, and that the nature of the game, with its particular traditions, seemed to attract 'authoritarian personality types'.[37] These corollaries are not without significance for Afrikaner nationalism; they reinforced values like respect for perceived tradition, rules and authority, integral to the nationalist movement, and at the same time encouraged a certain cultural conformity.

As a form of popular culture, rugby had considerable self-generating power, but it also needed to be recharged by outside currents in the form of touring teams. Such teams often received tumultuous welcomes and almost saturation media coverage. During the 1970 tour of New Zealand to South Africa, Laidlaw found that

> *the All Blacks were pictured, pestered, pondered, prodded*
> *and praised until every man, woman and child knew that this*
> *player ate eggs for breakfast, that one ate spinach, this*
> *lock-forward visited the toilet twice a day, and that one*
> *twenty times.*[38]

Rugby tours by overseas countries provided a focal point for national interest, an opportunity to showcase a 'sanitised' South Africa during the first decades of apartheid and, perhaps more importantly, to demonstrate that the Afrikaner could beat the best the world could offer. Cultural entrepreneurs explicitly stated that such events were important for promoting ethnic self-esteem.[39]

Rugby's considerable spectator appeal – for example, the 1955 tour of the British Lions was watched by record-breaking crowds – further contributed to a common consciousness. Interest in rugby can be seen as one element contributing to the shaping of what Benedict Anderson, in a memorable phrase, has called 'an imagined community'.[40] One is hard-pressed to find a clearer expression of this sense of community and the fusion of the private and public worlds than in the official message of Danie Craven upon the occasion of the 75th anniversary of the South African Rugby Board in 1964:

> *South Africa, this is your celebration, your festival, for the*
> *game belongs to you ... You have seen bright and dark days,*
> *smiles and tears; you have experienced tension and gaiety;*
> *certainty and uncertainty, but they have made you stronger*
> *and nobler. They have welded you together as nothing else*
> *in our history; and it has been this game which has provided*
> *you with a feeling of belongingness, of a oneness which so*
> *few people ever feel. It has taken you away from your own*
> *world into a larger world ... it has given you friends ...*[41]

Shared sporting enthusiasms hold out the strong possibility of sharing other wider interests as well. In this respect, Eric Hobsbawm has neatly outlined the role of sport in the formulation of a nationalistic consciousness:

> *What has made sport so uniquely effective a medium for inculcating national feelings, at all events for males, is the ease with which even the least political or public individual can identify with the nation as symbolised by young persons excelling at what practically every man wants, or at one time in life has wanted, to be good at. The imagined community of millions seems more real as a team of 11 named people. The individual, even the one who only cheers, becomes a symbol of his nation himself.*[42]

In South Africa, rugby performed precisely this function of merging and strengthening affinities. In this sense, the game can be seen as a powerful, if informal, disseminator of nationalist sentiment and a source of identification with the *volk* at large. For outside visitors to the country, the neat fit between nationalist politics and rugby as an integral element of Afrikaner popular culture was a distinct feature of the social landscape.[43]

Equally pertinent is the way in which an attempt was made to indigenise and 'Afrikanerise' the culture surrounding rugby. One area in which this found expression was the widespread practice of assigning nicknames to prominent players. Nicknames in sport are, of course, not uncommon. They often serve the purpose of decreasing the psychological distance between the successful performer and the average spectator. It can be seen as a symbolic way of 'cutting a player down to the size of ordinary people', and drawing the player into a private world of the familiar and the commonplace.[44] What is particularly noticeable about rugby nicknames in South Africa is the way in which they reflect an Afrikaner rural background. Approximately 60 per cent of recorded nicknames have rural or related connotations. 'Jakkals' (jackal) Keevy, 'Hasie' (bunny) Versfeldt, 'Koei' (cow) Brink, 'Skilpad' (tortoise) Eloff, 'Padda' (frog) Melville, 'Apie' (monkey) Pretorius, 'Appels' (apples) Odendaal, 'Wa' (wagon) Lamprecht, and 'Boon' (bean) Rautenbach were just a few of the names Afrikaner rugby enthusiasts affectionately bestowed on players.[45] The rural imagery evoked by these names correlated with a dimension of Afrikaner nationalism which had, as its representational theme, the notion of Afrikaners as solid, pioneering men of the soil, subsumed under the honorary title '*boere*'.[46] On the basis of this, it is not inconceivable that inter-locking emblematic themes, drawing upon the familiar, acted as a further factor blending nationalism and rugby in the public mind.

Afrikanerdom and rugby politics

The question of nationalism and control over the game was closely linked. The Second World War proved to be the catalyst for highlighting this inter-relationship. The decision of the United Party government to participate in the Second World War in 1939 had a deeply divisive effect on the white community. A considerable number of nationalistic Afrikaners opposed South Africa's entry into the war, arguing that there was no need for South Africa to rush to the aid of the British, who from the days of the Anglo-Boer War of 1899 to 1902 were perceived by many Afrikaners as the traditional 'enemy'.

These antagonisms spilled over onto the playing fields and clubs when predominantly English-speaking and pro-war administrators collected money for war funds during rugby fixtures and organised games with the specific aim of boosting the war coffers. The anti-war faction retaliated by organising games on behalf of the *Reddingsdaadbond*, an Afrikaner organisation which ostensibly collected funds for 'poor white' Afrikaners. This added fuel to the fire, with some rugby unions – most notably Eastern Province and Western Province – being split right down the middle. Dissidents, incensed that rugby should be used to support the war effort, formed their own unions and arranged their own games. Rugby was now divided along pro-war and anti-war lines and the schism had a rough English-Afrikaans correlate.[47]

At the rugby-playing Mecca, the University of Stellenbosch, it was claimed that the club had no option but to break away because the Western Province Union had decided to introduce politics into sport. Conveniently ignoring that the establishment of their own union was equally political, the legendary and influential A.F. Markötter argued that rugby was of greater importance than any other possible concern. Upon leaving the Western Province Union, he exclaimed: 'Mr Chairman, I have no religion. I have no politics. My religion and politics are rugby. You will not stop Stellenbosch from playing rugby.'[48]

Although the divisions were serious enough at the time, once South Africa's involvement in the war had ended in 1945, it was possible in the less volatile post-war political atmosphere to work towards a reconciliation between the two factions. After patient negotiations, the breakaway clubs were eventually unconditionally admitted back into the fold.[49] To all intents and purposes, quiet had returned to the rugby front in 1945, but much of it was illusory since the thorny question of political control of the sport remained. Although Afrikaners had taken to rugby in large numbers, they had yet to capture the administration of the game and dictate its politics. Commenting on the emotions engendered by the divisions of the war years, A.J. Pienaar, President of the South African Rugby Board, noted:

Dissident clubs should remember that rugby football was really an English game, introduced by English pioneers, and fostered in this country by all sections of the community, English, Afrikaans, Jews, Gentiles and coloured people, and that the dissident's views were not the only views that could be expressed or respected.[50]

Although unintended, implicit in this was an important message for Afrikaners: unless they had full control of the various bodies involved in rugby, they would be unable to influence the wider social and political dimensions of the sport in South Africa.

Afrikanerisation of the rugby establishment was a slow process. In the Transvaal it took at least 20 years for Afrikaners to gain ultimate control of the union. Attempts had already been made in the mid-1940s to oust English speakers from the administration of the union, but it was only in 1965 that J. le Roux was able to take the reins from the long-serving H.J. Sanderson, as the first Afrikaner president of the Transvaal Rugby Union. Le Roux's election was preceded by an intensive campaign to influence various clubs and to ensure that members with Afrikaner sympathies were well placed in the organisational structure of the union. Le Roux's victory did not come as a bolt from the blue; it was carefully orchestrated and meticulously planned. Nothing was left to chance: on the eve of the election arrangements were even made with the employer of a 'doubtful' member who, it was suspected, might vote against the Afrikaner faction, to send him out of town on 'business' on the crucial day to ensure that he would not be able to cast his vote.[51]

Of undoubted importance in bringing about Afrikaner control of the rugby administration was the *Afrikaner Broederbond* (the Brotherhood). The *Broederbond* was a secret, ostensibly cultural organisation consisting of elite Afrikaners. It worked ceaselessly to promote exclusively Afrikaner interests in different levels of society. Rugby being considered the 'national' game of the Afrikaner, it is not surprising to find that, over the years, the *Broederbond* gained significant influence in the rugby unions.[52]

What is surprising, however, is that Danie Craven, chairman of the South African Rugby Board from 1956 on, was not a member of the *Broederbond*. Why was such an important position entrusted to a non-Broeder? Part of the answer is that even though the *Broederbond* was powerful, it was not omnipotent. Craven, through his long association with rugby in South Africa and his overseas contacts, and by virtue of his forceful personality, managed to attract support from *Broeder* and non-*Broeder* alike. Ousting Craven and installing a *Broeder* would have called for an exceptional effort and a unique candidate to match Craven's credentials. It seems, too, that in broad ideological terms, the *Broederbond* was able to live with Craven. While he was more pragmatic and less purist than most *Broeders*, the division between Craven and the *Broederbond* was not unbridgeable. Craven had grown used to dealing with *Broeders* at the University of Stellenbosch, and the rugby world was no different. This does not imply that the two parties trusted each other whole-heartedly. Craven made it clear that he would not tolerate undue interference in rugby affairs by the *Broederbond*. In turn, at the time of the South African tour to New Zealand in 1956 with Craven as manager, there were widespread rumours that the *Broederbond* had seen to it that D. de Villiers, a *Broeder*, was appointed as assistant manager with the deliberate intention that he should keep a watchful eye on Craven.[53]

While Afrikaner control over the administration of rugby was well established in the 1960s, changes in the social composition of Afrikanerdom began to affect the popularity of rugby as the main, and often only, sporting pursuit of young Afrikaner men. These changes were related to a booming economy and the increasing embourgeoisement of Afrikaners. The South African economy registered a real growth rate of 8,1 per cent in 1963, 6,7 per cent in 1964 and 6,6 per cent in 1965. More and more Afrikaners had come to excel at business and in the professions, and along with their domination of the civil service as an almost exclusive preserve, they gained in confidence and social self- expression. They no longer felt inferior to English speakers. With greater wealth at their disposal and a modified self-image, it was possible to embrace more varied leisure-time interests. Sports such as swimming, cricket, golf and tennis slowly began to compete with rugby.[54] It was with some unease that the rugby establishment commented upon these trends. The youth, it was claimed in 1968, was becoming 'soft' and 'King Rugby' ran the risk of becoming a third-rate sport in South Africa.[55] It was an unduly pessimistic view. Although social developments did affect rugby, the game had over the years built up too much support among Afrikaners to be seriously threatened. The linkages between Afrikaner nationalism and rugby might have become slightly more tenuous, but they were not in any danger of being severed. Rugby's real challenge in the late 1960s was not to come from changing social patterns among Afrikaners, but from an Afrikaner government intent on the rigid application of apartheid regulations.

Apartheid was more than a system of legally entrenched racial discrimination; it also completely skewed the distribution of access to resources. Facilities for whites were far superior to those of blacks. This gave the lie to the often-quoted claim that apartheid provided 'separate but equal' opportunities. Having made rugby its 'national' game, the Afrikaner establishment had little concern for the rugby being played by other population groups. Although black rugby had a long history in the Eastern Cape (where missionary influence coupled with the zeal of new rugby converts carried the ball from the late 19th century through to the 1960s), its unions functioned separately from the white ones.[56] The inequality between white and black rugby was graphically reflected in the contrasting conditions in which the game was played. Mono Badela, a well-known figure in Eastern Cape black rugby circles, highlighted these:

> Talk South African rugby, and the images which spring to mind are fairly obvious. Sweaty white men in green jerseys. Springbok badges on their chests. Titanic battles on the plush green grass of Ellis Park, Loftus Versfeldt or Newlands. Currie Cup fever, tours to Australia, France and England ... The pictures are vivid and clear ... but there is another side to South African rugby – the game played in the dusty Eastern Cape townships of New Brighton, Mdantsane, Kwazakhele and Zwidi. There, the images are of dilapidated stadiums which look more like cross-country courses than playing fields. Scenes of African and coloured working class people, scrumming down on a dusty stony surface, car headlights illuminating a cold winter's night.[57]

In the 1960s rugby, like almost everything else in South Africa, was strictly segregated. No 'mixed' teams, and no matches between black and white teams were allowed. Prime Minister Hendrik Verwoerd, whose name has become synonymous with the period of high apartheid, was not prepared to grant any concessions on this score – even if it involved jeopardising the chances of international tours to South Africa. His announcement to this effect in 1965 effectively scuttled the 1967 All Black tour of South Africa, which would have included some Maoris.

After Verwoerd's assassination in 1966, his successor, B.J. Vorster, relented somewhat. Vorster, himself having been active in rugby administration in the Eastern Cape during the war years, was sensitive to the importance of rugby as a flag bearer of Afrikaner nationalism in the international arena. Even so, his decision to allow so-called 'non-whites' in foreign teams to play in South Africa met with opposition from within and contributed to the breakaway of a few National Party members of parliament to form the *Herstigte* (Reformed) National Party in 1969. While Vorster had opened the way for the 1970 All Black tour to South Africa, which contained three Maoris and one Samoan, his 'largesse' did not extend to cricket, and an English cricket team with a former South African coloured player, Basil D'Oliviera, was not allowed to play in South Africa.

Vorster argued, rather unconvincingly, that D'Oliviera's selection was not based on merit and that he had been deliberately chosen to embarrass the South African government.[58] What is revealing is that Vorster seems to have been more concerned about the international stature of rugby, the premier Afrikaner sport, than that of cricket, a game played mainly by English speakers and one at which few Afrikaners excelled at international level at that time. Narrow ethnic considerations seem to have been a factor in permitting concessions for rugby, but not for cricket. It is also likely that, at a time of increasing political pressure from those opposed to 'mixed' tours, Vorster was keen to placate such elements and willing to sacrifice cricket (but not rugby) in the process.

The end of the 1960s was a turning-point as far as South African rugby relations were concerned. Nothing made this clearer than the 1969-70 tour to Great Britain. Under the guidance of Peter Hain, who had been to school in South Africa, an assortment of anti-apartheid organisations launched large-scale demonstrations against the tour. Through various disruptive tactics they came close to forcing the South African management to disband the tour. In South Africa the conduct of the demonstrators was met with stunned indignation. It was unheard of that the cream of South African rugby should be humiliated and insulted by demonstrators whom the Afrikaans press often described as 'long- haired, unwashed, drug-taking, communist agitators'. Under these circumstances, nothing gave the Afrikaner rugby public more pleasure than when Mannetjies Roux, a backline replacement, impetuously and unceremoniously kicked a demonstrator in the pants during a pitch invasion at Coventry – an act which immediately elevated the already popular Roux to the ranks of a folk hero among Afrikaners.[59]

On the return of the South African team from the demo-ridden tour, Danie Craven declared:

> We despise the conduct of the demonstrators, the way in which rugby matches were turned into chaos, the childishness and banalities of the demonstrators. We would like to put it clearly and openly that if these people think that they can influence us or that we shall change our way of life because of demonstrations, they are making a grave error.[60]

As the subsequent two decades proved, Craven was wrong. The apartheid order came under serious threat from within and without, and sport isolation certainly played a part, though not necessarily a decisive one, in bringing this about. During this period Afrikanerdom had to choose between its racial politics and international rugby. It was reluctant to make the choice, and it was only in 1990, with the unbanning of political organisations, that the choice was made and that South African rugby was welcomed back into the international fold.

Rugby and masculinity

Much of Afrikaner historiography dealing with the history of the *volk* has been predominantly 'conceived of in terms of male actors who create and sustain the nation by military and constitutional or political struggles from which women were by definition excluded'.[61] Such an approach is problematical on three counts: it renders women historically invisible; as a natural corollary it contains no conception of gender relations; and the understanding of nationalism and the *volk* is restricted to the political, thus lacking inter-locking social and cultural dimensions.

Rugby is an arena where not only nationalism is played out in a particular way; gender relations are also influenced and reinforced. Rugby, in part at least because of the rough, physical nature of the game, has acquired a reputation of being pre-eminently 'a man's game'. It has been described as the 'ultimate man-maker', inculcating values such as 'courage, self-control and stamina'. All of these, it is claimed, are the products of the 'man-to-man' element in rugby, for to 'play rugger well, you must play it fiercely, and at the same time, and all the time, remember while doing so that you are a gentleman'.[62] From a very young age, boys in rugby-playing countries have been socialised into a world where rugby is an important element in the construction of male identity. Although some boys might have spurned the narrow basis upon which male identity was defined, the culture of the sport, imbued with a strong sense of tradition, encouraged conformity. The presumed connection between rugby and manliness was often woven into father-son relationships. An evocative illustration of this ritual transmission is to be found in many photographs of primary school rugby: 'A real lineout on a full-size field of little boys with bewildered expressions, knobbly knees, and spindly arms, all in real uniforms and short hair. Savage-looking parents patrol the sideline.'[63]

The association between rugby and manliness was often carried over from youth to adulthood, and it was also reinforced off the playing field through the practices and rituals which became part of the rugby-playing community. One such South African practice worth recounting is that of *borselling*: the team lifts one of the members chest-high and beats him on the backside with bare hands.[64] For some it was meant to be a form of initiation; for others who had transgressed the rules of a touring party it was a form of punishment. But there is also a sense in which this act can be seen as promoting team cohesion and therefore, implicitly, firmer male bonding.

Apart from the players whose 'maleness' could find forceful expression on rugby tours, the game also offered male spectators an opportunity of celebrating, however briefly, a collective manhood. A journalist has recalled the importance that watching rugby at Newlands in Cape Town had for her father in the 1950s and early 1960s:

For him it was a vicarious pleasure, a dream of camaraderie and manhood that assured him an escape into a world of physical splendour that was reasonably cheerful and brotherly, a sort of war with rules, and oranges to suck at half-time.[65]

Since the game was such an overpowering male activity, where 'maleness' mattered above all else, it is not surprising that because of inadequate contact with members of the opposite sex some rugby men were inclined to stereotype women. Thus, Danie Craven's view of women was that they 'should be soft, soft by nature, soft by word of mouth. If they are not soft, they simply do not have influence over a man'. Craven, and probably a host of other young sportsmen of his generation, also tended to shy away from casual affairs. 'I got to know women late,' he told a journalist in the mid-1980s.

Do you know, my dear, I went on four overseas tours and never had a woman. I now think I was a bloody fool, but do you know that my rugby meant so much to me that I thought in those days that if I had a woman it would affect my game, that it would be unfair to my country.[66]

While Craven's views reflect an outlook usually associated with perceived Victorian values of an earlier era, changing social and sexual mores of later decades brought about corresponding changes in the attitudes of rugby players towards women. Writing approximately 35 years after Craven's playing days, Chris Laidlaw, who came to South Africa with the All Blacks in 1970, had this to say:

Unlike beer, women on tour are not compulsory. Sometimes taken, sometimes left, they are a commodity to be utilised only if instantly available and free, which they usually are, in considerable plentitude. The sex scene on rugby tours is a woman's liberationist's nightmare.[67]

Besides the attitudes and behaviour of some rugby players on tour, it is also instructive to look at the conduct of rugby enthusiasts in general. An incident which took place in the mid-1960s is particularly revealing since it incorporates and reflects upon a range of attitudes. A journalist has recounted that on the morning before a test match to be played at Ellis Park in Johannesburg, crowds of white men were queuing for standing room. Many of them had had a fair amount of alcohol, and they started pelting black passersby with *naartjies* (small oranges). To the great merriment of the crowd, the blacks dropped whatever they had with them and quickly retreated in the opposite direction – all of them, that is, but a solitary black woman.

She was fashionably attired with high-heel shoes, make-up and a wig. She summed up the situation, gripped her handbag and strutted past the men. Incensed by such defiance, the men grabbed fistfuls of *naartjies* and bombarded her. One *naartjie* dislodged her wig to reveal a cleanly shaven head. The men fell about in paroxysms of laughter. But without any outward show of emotion, she picked up the wig, dusted it, reached into her handbag to find a vanity mirror, and calmly and coolly replaced and adjusted the wig. Proudly and apparently unperturbed, she went on her way.[68]

This incident demonstrates attitudes deeply rooted in class, race and gender antagonisms. The fact that the woman was smartly dressed, in clothes that were probably more expensive than many white women could afford, was one reason why the ire of the crowd was aroused. In her dress she conveyed an upper middle class image which made the men suspect she had ideas above her station. Even more visible, and perhaps more important, was the issue of race. At the height of apartheid in the mid-1960s, the dignity of many blacks had been stripped away along with their citizenship. Many whites were inclined to interpret assertive behaviour on the part of black people as deliberately provocative. For a black person to challenge white supremacist notions in everyday life, especially at Ellis Park and at such a moment, was to open the flood gates of racism. On top of this, the fact that it was a woman who was daring to breach the barricades of a demarcated male public space aroused even greater indignation. Symbolically then, what the woman represented was anathema to an inebriated male crowd. As far as the woman herself was concerned, her individual act of defiance had parallels in the history of the political struggle of black women against apartheid.[69]

In analysing the way gender was refracted through rugby, one also has to account for women who, with apparent enthusiasm, attended rugby matches as spectators. Afrikaner women at Stellenbosch in the 1930s and 1940s attended games and for many of them rugby on Saturdays was a major social occasion.[70] In later years, the importance of having women spectators at rugby matches was officially endorsed

by the South African Rugby Board. 'The school girl of today is a
spectator of tomorrow', it was said in 1968.

They will have their families, and if they are rugby ...
women, their children will be also ... We who attended
mixed [co- educational] schools know what an important
role girls played in our rugby lives and how important rugby
was to them too.[71]

It is not difficult to detect the male assumptions in the position outlined
by the South African Rugby Board. Women were welcomed into fold
because it served the interest of men and of the sport in general. This
is not to deny that some women might have had a genuine interest in
the game, and in all likelihood male rugby heroes were also their
heroes. Structurally, however, because rugby was such a dominantly
male activity, entry into that world, wittingly or unwittingly, could
only be on terms predetermined by men. This situation was similar to
the place of women in the political mobilisation of Afrikanerdom in
the 1930s and 1940s; the ideal of the *volksmoeder* (mother of the
nation) at the time meant that women could only gain social recognition as participants in the lives of their husbands and children.[72]

It is in the area of gender relations that the question of continuity
and discontinuity in the transmitting and appropriating of a sporting
culture manifests itself most pertinently. While Afrikaner nationalists
attempted, in some respects successfully, to 'Afrikanerise' an imperial sport like rugby, the 'maleness' of the sport – an historical
hallmark of the game in the metropole – was left intact. It was one of
the aspects of imperial rugby culture which Afrikaners adopted and
even reinforced without a further thought. Ultimately this demonstrates that the transformation of a sporting culture is seldom complete
– traces and even substantial elements of the old will be incorporated
into the new. It also points to the complexities of interpretation in
dealing with the issue of sport in a colonial setting. 'Where does the
promoting hand of the colonial master stop and where does the
adapting and assimilating indigenous tradition start?' is the intriguing
and tantalising question.[73]

Conclusion

In 1989 Tommy Bedford, one of the few English-speaking Springbok captains since 1960, commented critically on the rugby establishment and claimed that over a period of 25 years, it had worked 'mainly to promote the Afrikaner, his Church, his Party, his Government and the *Broederbond*, but all of it was to the detriment of rugby, sport and South Africa'.[74] This situation, somewhat bluntly described by Bedford, was the outcome of a more complex historical process.

The dynamics of this development, it has been suggested in this chapter, are to be found in the important role played by the University of Stellenbosch, the coupling of rugby symbolism and ethnic nationalism, the middle class character of the sport, the spectator appeal of rugby and its ramifications – including gender implications – and the reinforcement of notions of masculinity, and ultimately effective political control of the game. These factors combined to elevate rugby into the Afrikaners' 'national sport'. Even so, the transformation was not complete. In regard to the essential 'maleness' and middle class character of the game, much of the older imperial ethos was retained.

Although no sport is ideological *per se*, the values and norms invested in and associated with rugby, or any other sport, can and often do make it ideological. Afrikaner appropriation of the game in South Africa, coinciding with general Afrikaner nationalistic political ascendancy, was in the final analysis a way of demonstrating and representing a specific brand of ideological power. For this reason, it also set itself up for attack by opposing political forces after 1969.

Notes

1.   D. Kotze (ed), *Professor HB Thom* (Stellenbosch, 1969), pp.78-79 (translation).
2.   F.J.G van der Merwe, 'Sport and games in Boer prisoner-of-war camps during the Anglo-Boer War, 1899-1902', *International Journal of the History of Sport*, 9 (3) December 1992, p. 442.
3.   R. Archer and A.Bouillon, *The South African game: sport and racism* (London, 1982) p. 69.
4.   B. Booyens, 'Studentelewe – die jongste tydperk', H.B.Thom (ed), *Stellenbosch, 1866-1966: Honderd jaar hoër onderwys* (Stellenbosch, 1966) p. 394 (quotation translated).
5.   Booysens, *Studentelewe* p. 394.

6.   *Rugby*, June 1974, p. 39 (quotation translated).
7.   D. Craven, "n Eeu van sport', Thom (ed), *Stellenbosch*, p. 431 (quotation translated).
8.   F. van Zyl Slabbert, *The last white parliament* (Johannesburg, 1985) p. 20.
9.   *Vigor*, December 1955, p. 36.
10. A.C. Parker, *Giants of South African rugby* (Cape Town, 1956) p. 57.
11. Compare D.H. Heydendrych, *Tukkie Rugby 75*, (Pretoria, 1983) pp. 4-20.
12. F.J. Nöthling, 'The pioneering years' in M.C. van Zyl (ed), *Northern Transvaal Rugby 50* (Pretoria, 1988) pp. 18, 22; I.P.W. Pretorius, 'Senior rugby in Pretoria, 1938-1989' (unpublished MA dissertation, University of South Africa, 1989) p. 21.
13. Quoted in Nöthling, 'The pioneering years' in Van Zyl (ed), *Northern Transvaal Rugby* p. 25.
14. E. Dunning, 'The development of modern football' in E. Dunning (ed), *The sociology of sport: a selection of readings* (London, 1971) p. 147.
15. Compare J.J. Fourie, *Afrikaners in die goudstad, 1886-1924* (Johannesburg, 1979) p. 166.
16. Quoted in P. Dobson, *Rugby in South Africa: A history, 1861-1988* (Cape Town, 1989) p. 89.
17. *Who's who in the Sporting World: Witwatersrand and Victoria: Rugby* (Johannesburg, 1933) pp. 2-3; South African Rugby Board Minutes, 1, Report on the 1912 tour to the United Kingdom, 6 February 1913.
18. *The Guardian Weekly*, 9-15 October 1992.
19. For the nature of Afrikaner nationalism see D. Moodie, *The rise of Afrikanerdom: power, apartheid and the Afrikaner civil religion* (Berkeley, 1975); H. Adam and H. Giliomee, *The rise of Afrikaner power* (Cape Town, 1979); D. O'Meara, *Volkskapitalisme: Class, capital and ideology in the development of Afrikaner nationalism, 1934-1948* (Johannesburg, 1983).
20. For the 1938 centenary celebrations see A. Grundlingh and H. Sapire, 'From feverish festival to repetitive ritual? The changing fortunes of Great Trek mythology in an industrialising South Africa, 1938-1989', *South African Historical Journal*, 21, 1989, pp. 19-27.
21. P.W. Grobbelaar (red), *Die Afrikaner en sy kultuur: Ons volksfeeste* (Cape Town, 1975) p. 219.
22. Archer and Bouillon, *The South African game*, p. 66.
23. Quoted in W. Roger, *Old heroes: The 1956 Springbok tour and the lives beyond* (London, 1991) p. 32.
24. R. Holt, *Sport and the British: a modern history* (Oxford, 1989) pp. 228-229.
25. J.G. Kellas, *The politics of nationalism and ethnicity* (London, 1991) p. 21.
26. Quoted in Archer and Bouillon, *The South African game*, p. 73.
27. Compare Booysens, 'Studentelewe' p. 364.
28. B. Booyens, *Danie Craven* (Cape Town, 1975) pp. 152-160.
29. D.Craven, *Die Leeus keil ons op* (Johannesburg, 1956) p. 62.

30. South African Rugby Board Minutes, 4, Meeting with Mr G. Hogg, 10 April 1957.

31. *The Sportsman*, March 1966, p. 12.

32. J.G. Williams, 'Sosiologiese ondersoek na bepaalde aspekte van die maatskaplike milieu en leefwyse van 'n groep provinsiale rugbyspelers' (unpublished MA dissertation, University of Pretoria, 1976) pp. 22-23.

33. W.G. le Roux, 'Die vermaaklikheid en ontspanning van die armblanke kind in Kaapstad' (unpublished MA dissertation, University of Stellenbosch, 1940) p. 82 and *passim.*

34. On soccer in South Africa see T. Couzens, 'An introduction to the history of football in South Africa' in B. Bozzoli (ed), *Town and countryside in the Transvaal* (Johannesburg, 1983) pp. 198-214; F.J. Nöthling, 'Soccer in South Africa: a brief outline', *Kleio*, 1982, pp. 28-41; I. Jeffrey, 'Street rivalry and patron-managers: football in Sharpeville, 1943-1985', *African Studies*, 15 (1), 1992, pp. 68-94; Archer and Bouillon, *The South African game*, pp. 98-101, 195-198.

35. *Huisgenoot*, 27 May 1966, p. 30.

36. C. Laidlaw, *Mud in your eye: A worm's eye view of the changing world of rugby* (Cape Town, 1974) p. 6.

37. J.M. Coetzee in *Die Suid-Afrikaan*, August 1988, p. 4. See also Williams, 'Sosiologiese ondersoek' p. 55, for views on race.

38. Laidlaw, *Mud in your eye* pp. 97-98.

39. For example J.R. Albertyn *et al*, *Kerk en Stad* (Stellenbosch, 1948) p. 262.

40. B. Anderson, *Imagined communities: Reflections on the origins and spread of nationalism* (London, 1983) p. 15.

41. R. Johnstone and C. Neville, *Rugby in South Africa* (Cape Town, 1964) p. i.

42. E.J. Hobsbawm, *Nations and nationalism since 1780: Programme, myth and reality* (Cambridge, 1990) p. 143.

43. Roger, *Old heroes*, pp. 32-33.

44. Compare J.K. Skipper, 'The sociological significance of nicknames: the case of baseball players' in *Journal of Sport Behaviour*, 7 (1) February 1984, pp. 28-37; N. Petryszak, 'Spectator sports as an aspect of popular culture – an historical view', *Journal of Sport Behaviour*, 1 (1) February 1978, pp. 14-27. For nicknames in the Southern African context see P. Pearson, 'Function, familiarity or fun? Nicknames in Rehoboth, Namibia', African Studies Institute paper, University of the Witwatersrand, October 1988.

45. *Rugby*, February 1975, p. 38.

46. Compare Grundlingh and Sapire, 'From feverish festival' p. 25.

47. F.J.G. van der Merwe, 'Afrikaner nationalism and sport', *Canadian Journal of Sport*, XXII (2) December 1991, pp. 40-42; G.B. Saaiman, 'Sport en politiek: Suid-Afrika se sportisolasie en die invloed op die binnelandse politiek', unpublished MA dissertation, University of the Orange Free State, 1981, pp. 106-108; G. Kotze, *Sport en politiek* (Pretoria, 1978) pp. 11-20; Dobson, *Rugby in South Africa* pp. 85-89.

48. Quoted in D.H. Craven, *Oubaas Mark* (Cape Town, 1959) p. 193.

49. Dobson, *Rugby in South Africa* p. 92.

50. South African Rugby Board Minutes, 2, 17 May 1943.

51. Kotze, *Sport en politiek*, pp. 11-28.

52. I. Wilkins and H. Strydom, *The Super-Afrikaners* (Johannesburg, 1978) p. 245.

53. T. Patridge, *A life in rugby* (Johannesburg, 1991) pp. 70-73; Roger, *Old heroes* p. 90; Kotze, *Sport en politiek* p. 121; P. Dobson, *Doc: The life of Danie Craven* (Cape Town, 1994) pp. 133-135. I am also indebted to Lappe Laubscher for comments on the relationship between Craven and the *Broederbond*. The interpretation, however, is my own.

54. D. Welsh, 'Urbanisation and the solidarity of Afrikaner nationalism', *Journal of Modern African Studies*, 7 (2) 1969 pp. 265-276; W. Beinart, 'South Africa in the 20th century', unpublished manuscript, unpaginated.

55. South African Rugby Board, 4, President's report, 1968. See also *Die Huisgenoot*, 27 May 1966.

56. For a history of black rugby see J.B. Peires, '*Facta non verba*: Towards a history of black rugby in the Eastern Cape' unpublished paper, History Workshop, University of the Witwatersrand, 1981; Dobson, *Rugby in South Africa* pp. 167-227.

57. M. Badela, 'Scrumming down', *Leadership*, 12 (5) 1993, p. 117.

58. R.E. Lapchick, 'The politics of race and international sport: the case of South Africa', unpublished D.Phil. thesis, University of Denver, 1973, pp. 147-150, 179-184, 247, 252-253; Kotze, *Sport en politiek* pp. 51-79; Archer and Bouillon, *The South African game* p. 74; R. Thompson, *Retreat from apartheid: New Zealand's sporting contacts with South Africa* (Wellington, 1975) pp. 35-42.

59. Lapchick, 'The politics of race' pp. 304-318; Kotze, *Sport en politiek* pp. 125-131; Dobson, *Rugby in South Africa* p. 132; *Die Beeld*, 9 November 1969. (Quotations translated from the latter source).

60. Quoted in Booyens, *Craven*, p. 183. (Quotation translated).

61. D. Gaitskell, J. Kimble and E.Unterhalter, 'Historiography in the 1970s: A feminist perspective', *Southern African Studies: retrospect and prospect*, Centre of African Studies, University of Edinburgh, p. 164.

62. E.H.D. Sewell, *Rugger – The Man's game* (London, 1950) p. 22.

63. M.N. Pearson, 'Heads in the sand: The 1956 Springbok tour to New Zealand in perspective' in R. Cashman and M. McKernan (eds), *Sport in history: the making of modern sporting history* (Sydney, 1979) p. 282.

64. Pearson, 'Heads in the sand', p. 285. See also Roger, *Old heroes*, p. 91; J. Robbie, *The game of my life* (London, 1989) p. 125.

65. L. Sampson, 'Yesterday's Heroes', in Anon, *Laughing through the turmoil* (Johannesburg, 1990) p. 49.

66. Sampson, 'Yesterday's Heroes', p. 50.

67. Laidlaw, *Mud in your eye* p. 58. See also Roger, *Old heroes* p. 90.

68. *Vrye Weekblad*, 4-10 October 1991, p.25.

69. See for example J. Wells, *We now demand: a history of women's resistance to pass laws in South Africa* (Johannesburg, 1992).

70. E. Theron, *Sonder hoed of handskoen* (Kaapstad, 1983) p. 83; Interview with Ms. B. Sieberhagen, a student at Stellenbosch during the 1930s and 1940s, 6 January 1994.

71. South African Rugby Board, 4, President's report, 1968.

72. E. Brink, 'Man-made women: Gender, class and ideology of the "volksmoeder"', in C. Walker (ed) *Woman and gender in South Africa* (Cape Town, 1990) p. 288.

73. R. Cashman, 'Cricket and colonialism: colonial hegemony and indigenous subversion?' in J.A. Mangan, *Pleasure, profit, proselytism: British culture and sport at home and abroad*, 1700-1914 (London, 1988) p. 261.

74. *Die Suid-Afrikaan*, December 1988-January 1989, p. 6.